Pricing for a Profit: Setting Your Rates as a Freelancer

Launching a Successful Freelance Business, Volume 3

Ashley Simpson

Published by Ashley Simpson, 2023.

While every precaution has been taken in the preparation of this book, the publisher assumes no responsibility for errors or omissions, or for damages resulting from the use of the information contained herein.

PRICING FOR A PROFIT: SETTING YOUR RATES AS A FREELANCER

First edition. November 24, 2023.

Copyright © 2023 Ashley Simpson.

ISBN: 979-8223597353

Written by Ashley Simpson.

Table of Contents

Introduction

There may be nothing more exciting than the moment you first score a big payday in your new freelance career. This isn't to say that freelancers live hand-to-mouth where they feel completely reliant on a paycheck to bide their time until the next round of bills is due. Instead, it is simply a testament to how good it feels to know that *you* made that money happen with a skill set that is unique to you. That first paycheck is a point of pride for most people, even if they don't live for the money itself. The question is: what is the number one thing you can do to ensure you have money rolling into your bank account week after week, month after month?

Perhaps the most important part of establishing a freelancing career is knowing how to set your rates so you get paid fairly and on time. Without a clear picture of what your rates need to be or how to charge for your services, you will never make the kind of lucrative living needed to pay your bills. Just because you are striking out on your own doesn't mean you need to charge minimum wage (or less). In fact, undercutting your competitors in this way doesn't reflect well on your business and may actually turn would-be clients away from your services. There is an idea out there (and maybe rightly so) that you get what you pay for, and this applies to freelancing just as much as any other area. Being the cheapest person in the marketplace is fine for some clients, but the good ones are willing to pay fair market value for the services you provide. The idea here is that you need to find more of these clients and let the others go so you can make an honest living on your own terms.

Sometimes, you might find that setting your rates low early in your career is strategic, but it isn't designed to be a long-term solution. This is a strategy I employed for my very first client, and it was arguably the only reason I got my foot in the door, collected a new five-star review, and scored some credibility with subsequent clients. I was writing short 500-word medical articles on the health effects of smoking, complete with scholarly resources and a bibliography of medical studies. Each one took me roughly an hour because I hadn't yet honed my writing skills, but I was paid by the project – which is the only way I recommend getting paid (more on this in a later chapter). That meant no matter how quickly I worked, I still only made five dollars per article. Payment by the project gives you an incentive to work faster, but I labored over these articles and gave each one a full hour.

Yes, you read that right. I worked for five dollars per hour on my very first freelancing job.

At that time, the minimum wage was a little over seven dollars an hour. A little quick math shows that I was working for about 70 percent of minimum wage. My client was getting a steal, even though my writing skills weren't perfect and I'm sure there was a more efficient way to find research than the painstaking methods I took. I enjoyed the work, mainly because it was my first real taste of freedom from corporate America, fast food joints, and ice cream parlors. I could work when and how I wanted from the comforts of home. The benefits of freelancing stood out to me from the very first moment I stumbled upon Upwork, and that brief taste made me want more. (If you aren't sure whether freelancing is right for you, I would encourage you to read the first book in this series, *Freelance Freedom*, where we dive into the mindset and advantages of freelancing.)

Despite how happy I was to be working from home or a local coffee shop, I quickly realized I wouldn't be able to sustain working for just five dollars an hour. I could easily get a job elsewhere that paid twelve dollars an hour, so I needed to reconsider my pricing model. The problem is there were no clear and easy answers about how much I should charge for the services I offered. I looked high and low on the internet and at the library for tips on how much I should charge and came up empty. That research led me to realize there was a huge gap in the market when it came to helping freelancers establish their businesses in the early days – and this book was born!

No matter if you are a newbie freelancer or a seasoned pro looking for some guidance on how you can make more, this book offers the practical guidance you need to max out the market. We will dive into setting your hourly rate (and why you may not want to charge hourly), how to handle requests for free work and discounts, and how to compare your prices to competitors. There are a lot of nuances to finding the perfect rates for your unique business, and there are no one-size-fits-all answers. Instead, we will customize your approach to setting your rates so you can get the amazing feeling of depositing your very first paycheck in your bank account. Rest assured you can sustain this business for the long haul.

The whole process starts with valuing your time and deciding what you need to live the life you desire. We will look at it through a lens of what you *need* and what you *want*, giving you ample room for growth as your skills and experience increase. Get ready to forecast your financial future and dive into this first chapter with me!

Valuing Your Time

My recommendation is that you choose not to work on an hourly basis, but establishing a rough idea of what you should make per hour provides a critical framework for establishing rates. In the next chapter, we will talk a little bit more about how to package your services to avoid this hourly conundrum. For now, we're going to go with the hourly model to help you think more clearly about what you need to make on a project to pay your bills, cover your overhead, and keep the wheels on your new business. I shared in the introduction how I worked my very first job for a mere five bucks an hour, and maybe this will be your strategy too. However, I realized after that first job that what I was charging wasn't sustainable, and I moved into this system for calculating rates. Grab a pen and paper (and a calculator) because we're about to do some serious math.

Valuing your time starts with forecasting how much you need to make to pay your bills as well as have a little bit left over to contribute to savings and investments. Think about both your fixed costs (mortgage, rent, car payment, etc.) and variable expenses that are within your control (restaurants, clothing, coffee, entertainment, etc.). If you need help breaking down spending to see what you actually need to make each month, I recommend pausing here and picking up the second book in this series, *Finances for Freelancers* (and the accompanying workbook). For those who have been tracking with me since the beginning, you already know what you need to earn to sustain your lifestyle at a bare minimum and how to thrive at best with significant contributions to your savings and future investments like retirement savings accounts.

I want you to have these numbers fixed in your mind. We are going to calculate an hourly rate for you to simply sustain yourself as well as an hourly rate for your ideal lifestyle. Write the number you need to make for each category at the top of a piece of paper. If your goal is to make a cool six figures in the future to rival your salary in corporate America, then be ambitious and jot it down. Maybe you want to work less and clear half of that so you can spend more time with your family. No matter what your goals are, they are going to be personal to *you*. There are no right or wrong answers here. Some people want to maximize their earnings while some people simply want to maximize their lifestyle. The calculations will work regardless of where you fall on the spectrum of earning.

Let's start with your lower number or the figure you need just to cover your bills. This is likely where you will want to start until you can build up a roster of well-paying clients, gather some good reviews from completed jobs, and hone your skills to justify charging more. Put the other piece of paper to the side for the time being, but we will come back and repeat a variation on this exercise in a moment. Now, I want you to think about how many hours you would like to work each week. Ideally, nobody wants to work more than four hours each week. However, this is the time to be as realistic about your time as you possibly can be. If you are coming from a job where you work fifty hours a week, maybe you intend to spend an equal amount of time hustling on your new freelancing career until things start to take off.

Freelancing can be an attractive idea for some people because it allows them to take time off to focus on their families. In this case, maybe you only want to work thirty hours a week. The point is to be realistic about how much time you can dedicate to building a business while still having a sense of balance with your other responsibilities. There is a degree of hustle inherent to starting a new business of any kind, so keep that in mind when you name the number of hours you want to work per week for this lower figure. Remember: you need a basic salary to cover your bills. Now, I want you to multiply the number of hours you want to work per week by 50 (one for almost every week of the year).

This is also a good time to point out that it is extremely unrealistic to think you are going to work every single week with no sick days or vacation days. If you aren't sure how much time you will want to take off for these incidentals, I would factor in ten days of each at however many hours you intend to work per day. If you only want to work five-hour days, then you will need to add 100 hours to the figure calculated in the last paragraph. You may have more or less time off, depending on the number of hours you have slated for each day. For those who already have vacations planned that may exceed these hours, make sure you add them up and contribute them to the total. These are hours you will still want to be paid for, so they should be worked into your annual salary and hourly rate.

By this point, you should have a clear picture of how much you want to make each year as well as the number of hours you intend to work this year. There is one more thing you will need to take into consideration: your hustle. Not every hour spent on your business is going to be a paid hour. The time you spend applying for jobs, searching job boards, and emailing clients is *not* going to be paid, but this is the time you will work on your business, so you should be paid for your grind. Factor in a few hours for this each week. I have found that a good rule of thumb for your grinding is to spend about an hour a day on these miscellaneous administrative tasks and submitting proposals on new jobs. Sometimes, this means you won't be able to work as many paid hours because you will be too busy grinding and building your business. If you haven't factored this into your work week, go back to the last section and revise how many paid hours you want to be working each week alongside these admin tasks. Add the revised number with your admin and job submission hours to figure out a realistic idea of how many hours you will spend each year on your business.

Now, this is the easiest part: all you have to do is divide your desired annual salary by the number of hours you will work on your business plus your off time. The formula should look like this for those of you who need a little help with the math:

Desired Annual Salary / (Hours worked + Vacation & Sick Time) = Hourly Rate

This is the bare minimum that you can afford to charge per hour in order to cover your bills and any overhead expenses you have on your business. That does *not* mean that you have to charge this number for every job just because it's all you need for a successful income. Instead, it serves as a benchmark you can use to measure your rates, see how you are aligning with financial goals, and spot room for growth. I want to bring up an important point here: if your rates are hovering at or around minimum wage, you need to set your sights higher. You are providing a specialized skill and will have other expenses to factor in that you didn't have at a full-time office job. You will take a hit on your income when you have to pay that 15.3 percent self-employment tax on your earnings each quarter. Account for *all* of your expenses when setting your minimum income, which is why I recommend going to the previous book in the series first.

With this basic number in mind, I want you to think about your ideal life next. Flip over to the other piece of paper where you wrote what you want to be earning well into the future. I hope this number is substantially higher than the bare minimum needed. However, another thing to think about is that you may not want to work as many hours in the future so you can have more free time which is the benefit of a freelance career. Recalculate how many hours you want to work for you to feel satisfied with your work and redo the calculation. Don't forget to factor in vacation time, which may be more plentiful when you have more discretionary income to spend on lavish trips. This allows you to refill your creative well. You might have a higher desired annual salary and lower hours worked with more vacation and sick time. With this in mind, your end calculation should be substantially higher than your hourly rate from the previous example. This gives you something to strive for.

Don't forget you need to pay your taxes and the money you earn is not yours and yours alone. It might seem like you're making a lot of money per hour, but those taxes will gobble up your earnings in a heartbeat. Make sure you have them factored into the baseline figure you use in these exercises. Freelancers who don't plan to pay their payroll taxes (if you have an S-Corp) or quarterly taxes (as a sole proprietor, partnership, or LLC) will be very disappointed and may even be in quite a bind when it comes to tax time at the end of the fiscal year. Again, if you need help to calculate how much you will owe in taxes, I recommend seeing the previous book in this series for a breakdown of what your self-employment taxes and income taxes will be. Always check with the IRS to ensure you are factoring yourself into the right tax bracket for your income and filing status. An accountant can also help you calculate this figure and maximize your tax deductions so you can keep more money in your pocket, but that is an issue for another time.

With that in mind, there are two ways you can now approach your desired hourly rate: you can go with the bare minimum in order to get your feet wet and start accumulating clients, or go with a figure that falls somewhere between the two extremes. The problem with charging the absolute minimum you can get away with is that you will eventually have to raise your rates to make this sustainable long-term. If your clients are recurring (meaning you will work with them month after month), you may find they are quite disgruntled if you raise your rates three months into your agreement. They get used to the idea of paying a lower rate and don't expect to have an increase in their bills. While we will talk about how to broach rate increases with clients in a later chapter, this may not be a strategy you want to use long-term. It's fine for one-time clients such as for a graphic designer who will only design one logo for a business. When the job is over, you can charge more on the next contract you secure without upsetting anyone by blowing their budget or forcing them to find a new freelancer.

Once you build up a little bit of experience on the platform of your choice, you might want to consider splitting the difference and charging in the middle. This is a great stepping stone to get to your desired income in the months and years ahead. As your reputation grows, continue to scale your income and reevaluate whether you should be earning more as you go. You may even find the original six-figure income you set for yourself could turn into a multiple six-figure income over the next five to ten years, especially if you launch an agency instead of working solely on your own. As each contract ends and you bid on a new job, increase your rates strategically to get yourself closer to the ideal number.

This exercise gives you a foundation for thinking about how you can charge for services of any kind, but it isn't the only thing you need to consider when setting rates. The next chapter will help you to get a more realistic idea of what you need to charge based on your overhead costs (including some you may not have thought about in this exercise). We're almost through this heavy math section and can move onto the art of pricing your services, so stick with me for just a little bit longer.

Covering Your Costs

In the last section, we considered your desired income to determine an estimated hourly rate that will get you where you want to be financially. This is the number you need to pay your personal bills, set aside some money into savings, and pay your taxes. However, it doesn't factor in any of the costs of actually running your business. Oftentimes, these costs are low for freelancers but they can add up quickly and they should be factored into what you are charging for services. Take some time to thumb through this chapter, note any expenses you might want to cover, and then add this figure to your desired annual income for a more realistic calculation. You will find your hourly rate will be higher once you factor in these costs which is why this section is a must-read before you start bidding on potential jobs.

Membership Fees

MEMBERSHIP FEES AREN'T necessarily something you *have* to pay for; there are some job boards that are designed for freelancers and remote workers that don't charge anything. Perhaps the two best-known sites that have free tiers are Upwork and Fiverr. Upwork is my own platform of choice for the payment protection it offers freelancers, the abundance of jobs, and the robust features offered. Find what works best for you as you launch your business. Memberships may give you access to more features to help you score more jobs. One of my favorites is a sneak peek at what others are charging for the same services. Upwork memberships start right around $10 per month and allow you to see the price range of other bids and get more access to bid on new jobs. You will most certainly find other job boards that are more expensive, as well as some that are free.

My recommendation is not to pay for every job board out there. Instead, I want you to pick one and stick with it for a while. This allows you to build up a reputation as a stellar freelancer because people do look at reviews before they make a hiring decision. It also allows you to keep up with all new job postings that might be interesting to you. If you have to check three or four different job boards to see the influx of new jobs (and there are new jobs every few minutes, depending on your area of expertise), you may miss out on being the early bird who gets the worm. Some clients will be interested in hiring quickly and will make a decision within hours. It will also quickly feel overwhelming to apply to every job that is a fit for your skills when you are trying out multiple platforms. Focus your efforts in these early days, save yourself some money, and build up a reputation you can be proud of.

Commission Rates

MEMBERSHIP FEES AREN'T the only cost associated with working on job boards. Most of them will take a percentage of your earnings as a commission for facilitating the transaction. Given that they hold funds in escrow for you, intervene in client disputes, and provide a space for you to work and find jobs, this money is often well-earned. That being said, some freelancers forget to factor in the percentage a platform will take when payment is rendered. This could prove to be a problem when it comes to covering your costs. If you are charging the bare minimum of what you need to pay your bills, you should absolutely recalculate with commission rates in mind.

For example, Upwork takes ten percent of your earnings on most contracts. They used to have a sliding scale based on how much you earned, but they have recently switched back to this system for the time being. Take your desired hourly rate and tack on ten percent (or whatever the platform you choose might charge). This covers your costs because those commissions will be taken out of your pay before they ever hit your bank account. Multiply your hourly rate by 1.10 to see what you need to cover a ten percent charge. Modify the number after the decimal point to reflect whatever commission fee your platform charges.

Marketing

SOME FREELANCERS PREFER not to work on online job boards and may work with local businesses or clients instead. If you want to leverage contacts in the community, you might need to factor in some marketing costs. For example, let's say that you want to become a content creator working on blogs for storage companies in your area (yes, you may want to be this specific when it comes to defining your niche). When you head out to meetings with local storage facilities, you should have marketing materials with you to share with the owners or marketing managers. This might be a folder with a well-designed price sheet, a sample of the work you provide, and a nice business card tucked into the folder. It might seem like paper is free and business cards are cheap, but if you hand out enough of them, you will realize that the cost adds up. Graphic designers and artists may have even more sunk costs in their marketing materials as printing out past designs requires a lot of ink and paper.

Online Presence

IS IT EVEN POSSIBLE to run a business these days without an online presence? No matter how you intend to market your services, you may want to invest in launching a website that contains your portfolio and examples of past work. A sleek web design gives clients a taste of what it might be like to work with you. This is a great place to share relevant experiences, testimonials, and reviews all in one convenient location. You can link to your website in job proposals as a way for prospective clients to learn more about you before they make a hiring decision. An online presence is professional and, to some extent, expected by many clients.

This is *not* to say you need to hire an expensive web designer to get something perfect and polished. If you have the budget for this or if web design is in your wheelhouse, then feel free to sink some costs into your website. I firmly believe most people can set up a website on their own using WordPress and hosting plans like Bluehost. There are tons of free templates you can easily modify, add your own images, and upload your portfolio. Plan to spend a few hours learning how to use your new website, but the actual design of it can be relatively inexpensive. You do need to factor in your hosting costs and domain name which may run you around $100 per year. Of course, there are other platforms that will be more user-friendly for the tech-challenged among us. Squarespace is one that will charge you monthly. It's a little more expensive but the drag-and-drop interface is super simple to use.

Social media can also be a powerful way to connect with other businesses and clients. At first glance, you might think this is free but many freelancers will want to reconsider. If this is the avenue you intend to use to find new clients, it might be beneficial to pay for some social media advertisements. It is getting harder and harder for businesses to show up in organic traffic in every niche. Factor in a small marketing budget to get your name out there and link back to your website as well as your social media. Take some time to research how much you might spend on this type of marketing based on your reach, who you want to target, and how specific you want to be based on geographical area.

Equipment

MANY PEOPLE ASSUME that they have everything they need to start a freelancing career. After all, most people will only need a laptop and some basic software to get their business off the ground. A photographer might need access to Adobe Photoshop and a nice DSLR camera while a graphic designer might need a tablet and access to Procreate or Adobe Illustrator. A writer needs even less: a laptop and an internet connection with Google Docs or Microsoft Office. Because most people already have a laptop at their disposal, they forget to factor in the cost of their equipment when it comes to their annual costs.

This is a major mistake because you will need to replace it at some point. Even the most advanced laptop will only run for so many hours before it needs to be replaced by a newer model – and that new model doesn't come cheap. Factor in the cost of replacing your equipment every year or two because it is an inevitable and expensive thing to consider. Of course, many software options are now monthly subscriptions in the cloud so it is easy to calculate how much you will spend each year and add this number to your desired annual income. If you don't have to replace your equipment this frequently, then you can keep more money in your business bank account for when you do need to replace it. It's a good insurance policy to have a little money set aside for incidentals like a repair or new equipment.

Working Space

SOME FREELANCERS RELISH the idea of working from a home office or their dining room table. This is certainly a way to save some money, but it isn't always easy for everyone to literally work from home because there are so many distractions with your family and housework. Does this sound a little too familiar to you? If so, you might find yourself heading to a co-working space or a small local café to open your laptop and get to work. Of course, there is a cost associated with working anywhere other than your home office.

Make sure you factor in what you will spend on coffee, a rental space at a co-working center, or a sandwich at Panera Bread if that's where you choose to work. Factor in how much you spend each time you go and how frequently you go, and then add that to your desired annual salary. Some of these costs are tax-deductible, but you should discuss them with your accountant at the end of the year to make sure you categorize spending correctly.

Hopefully, this gives you a little more insight into the hidden costs of running a successful business. You may have other categories of spending that need to be added to your desired annual salary to ensure you are *really* covering your costs and earning enough to pay your bills. From here, you can start to examine what other people in your industry are charging to get a better feel for where you want to set your hourly rate between what you need and what you ultimately want.

Price Comparisons

You know exactly what it costs to run your business and how much you *need* to make per hour for success. At this point, most people are wondering whether the market will really bear what they want or need to charge for services. You might be used to someone else dictating what you earn and having all of the costs of the business covered without a second thought. Your salary may have been lower as a result of the business taking those funds out of your paycheck before it ever hits your bank account. Where you may have earned $20 per hour at your day job, you now need to earn $35 to cover your bills, taxes, and overhead expenses associated with running a company of one (or more than one, if you open an agency). The question is: will people really pay this rate for your services?

Clients are often willing to pay more than we give them credit for which causes us to leave money on the table. If your client exclaims that your services are a bargain, this should be an indicator you need to raise your rates. Hiring a freelancer is a strategic move for a company that actually *saves* them money, even if they have to pay more than they would have to hire an in-house employee. Think about what it means to a company to be able to hire a freelancer instead of a full-time worker: they have to spend less on onboarding someone with training and orientation, they don't have to pay payroll taxes, and they don't have to manage benefits for someone new. As you likely have already seen in calculating your own expenses, all of these items might sound like they don't cost much, but the reality is different. Plus, clients may find they don't need a full-time worker because they only need a little help with a one-time project. Hiring and onboarding a new worker is time-consuming and expensive for a project that may only last for a few months or even less.

All of this is to say you should charge what you need to charge to achieve your idea of financial freedom. Some freelancers will still struggle to know what the market will bear in terms of their rates, so I encourage you to do a little price comparison with other similar freelancers or agencies that specialize in your area of expertise. A great way to do this is by simply calling around and asking what other local businesses are charging for services similar to yours. Graphic designers might call other design firms and ask what they charge for logo design. Approach this conversation as if you are a customer inquiring about services and rates. I would recommend calling five to ten places if this is the only research you will be doing. This tends to be the most nerve-wracking way to investigate what other people are charging. When picking up the phone makes you want to break out in hives, you can, fortunately, do a lot of this heavy lifting and research online.

First, you can look for websites of other freelancers or agencies who are offering similar services. Writers might look at content management websites to see what they are charging their clients for a short blog post or a technical paper. Designers might look at the packages and hourly rates set by other companies. Because most people have an online presence these days, it isn't all that hard to find a few comparable services and websites that promise a similar service and quality to what you can provide. If you have additional qualifications, extensive experience getting real results for clients, and some great testimonials to back up your work, you should be able to charge similar or even higher rates. This is just to give you an idea of what the going rate is; you can set your own rates however you need to in order to cover your expenses.

However, my usual method of comparing my going rates to the rates of others is to pay for a membership to Upwork. This is my preferred platform for freelancing, as mentioned earlier. By paying for their most basic membership, you gain access to see a range of what other people are bidding on a particular job. The price comparison feature doesn't allow you to see every individual bid, but you can see the lowest, highest, and average numbers. Chances are the lowest bid will be way out of the range you need to charge to cover your costs and salary. These platforms are often considered a race to the bottom, where some freelancers are willing to undercut others just in order to make a quick buck. You won't be able to compete with people who are charging much less than the figure you calculated in the last couple of chapters. With more people from overseas working on the platform, it can be hard to find a job that hasn't been underbid by someone in a country with a lower cost of living.

I don't advocate for ensuring you're the lowest person to bid on a job because clients are often willing to pay more than the bare minimum to get a job done right. For a beginner, I also don't recommend being the highest bid on a job because you may not have the experience or the reputation to warrant being paid top dollar – at least as far as your profile on sites like Upwork is concerned. You may have plenty of real-world experience, but this doesn't always translate to the platform until you have been around for a little while. The average tends to mean that your rates will blend into everyone else, so you really have two choices here: charge more than average or charge less than average. How do you decide which direction to go?

New freelancers may want to consider charging a little less than the average amount simply because they don't have much in the way of experience on the platform. A client has to be willing to take a risk on you because your reputation has yet to be proven. They might be more willing to take a chance on you if it seems like they are getting a real deal on your services. This might be a little less than your calculated hourly rate, which can be a little problematic. I recommend that you have some financial runway when you start freelancing, allowing you to take on low-paying clients that get you started. After all, some work is better than no work. It will help you grow your profile on the platform of your choice, earn you a little money to line your pockets, and give you a quick way to get into the freelancing game. Consider this price cut an investment in the long-term success of your brand and business.

When it seems like your hourly rate is going to have to be much higher than what other people are charging, you might want to reconsider your schedule. You could charge less per hour if you were willing to work more hours per week or per year (if you take fewer vacation and sick days). For some people, this is an easy fix to an expensive hourly rate. The more hours you have to work, the less you have to charge per hour in order to reach your goal. I'm not advocating for working yourself into the ground, but you may have to be more realistic if you thought you only wanted to work ten hours a week but needed to make $75,000 to cover your bills. An initial price cut might make you uncomfortable at first, but it can pay huge dividends just like my first five-dollar-an-hour job quickly turned into mid- to high-four-figure months for part-time work.

Once you have a few jobs under your belt, you might want to skew your rates toward the higher side of the average. You may be able to scale your income faster if you already have some experience in your niche and have a portfolio built up on a personal website or a lot of reach into your community. This lets clients know you provide an excellent service and are proud of the work you offer. Most understand that you get what you pay for sometimes and may be more willing to pay for services that are higher-end or premium compared to others. Eventually, you can start to price your services on the higher and higher end of the spectrum until you reach the point where the market will no longer bear your prices. When you bid on jobs consistently at these rates without nibbles on your proposals, it is a sign you are charging too much for most clients.

One of the nice features of Upwork is that you don't always have to compete with people who live in other countries. Sometimes, these freelancers from other countries can undercharge for their services because of a lower cost of living in their area. This is bad news for those based in an area with a higher cost of living like the United States or Europe. Some clients are willing to pay a premium price to hire a freelancer from the United States. They anticipate that the cost will be a bit higher, but it is easier to work with someone in the same time zones with English as a first language for easier and smoother communication. If you do intend to charge a higher hourly rate on one of these jobs, be careful to ensure that you are in the average range. It won't be as much of a race to the bottom and prices may be clustered closer together.

It's important to make sure you keep the prices of others in mind when bidding on jobs. It may be feasible for you to be the absolute lowest bid on your first couple of jobs – even if it means you will need to take a loss on them. As long as the projects aren't ongoing and you can really deliver on them in exchange for a positive review, it can be a good idea to take the loss. This is why someone was willing to take a chance on my services initially. I provided excellent value for a mere five dollars which sort of covered my costs. Undercutting other bids might be more feasible for those who are sticking with a full-time job while they build up a steady roster of clients.

The only word of caution I will throw out there is that some clients want too much for what you are charging. The scope of the project may change mid-project, making it unlikely you will be able to stick to the initial rates. Clients who change the scope of work may also be less likely to cover the costs of an increase in your rates. This jeopardizes your chances of getting that coveted five-star review which makes you more likely to land the next job. Having only one review on your profile can make people less likely to hire you, especially if that one review is less than positive. If you get any vibes from a client that they might be demanding, unrealistic, or want more than you can reasonably give for a low introductory rate, you are better off not taking the job. It may prove to be a nightmare you feel obligated to stick with in order to get a (very small) paycheck. Look for red flags in your initial conversations about the project and politely find a way to decline if you think it will be a nightmare job.

If you have made it this far, it's time to look at how you want to actually price your services. Some people might like to work hourly, but there are a number of drawbacks to this pricing method which is why I usually advocate for a rate based on the scope of the project. I'll explain why in the next chapter.

Hourly vs. Per Project Payments

You spent the last three chapters figuring out what you need to make on an hourly basis to cover your bills, and now I'm going to throw another wrench into the machine. Hourly isn't always the best system in order to cover your time costs and to help you make the most money on your new endeavor. Instead, I advocate for being paid on a per-project basis for several reasons. Let's take a deeper dive into the benefits of charging per project instead of hourly.

Faster Turnarounds, Same Profit

THE FIRST AND MOST important reason why I think all freelancers should charge for the service versus hourly is because they will eventually get faster at their craft. When you first get started, you might be like me and take a full hour to write 500 words. It might take you ten hours to design a set of logos for a brand or five hours to translate a five-page paper into another language. Once you get a little more proficient at your given trade, you will naturally take less time to complete it. Does that mean you should be paid less for the work you deliver?

Your clients are getting the same quality work if not something better than they received before. Just because it takes you less time to complete doesn't mean you have to charge them less for it. In fact, I would argue you could even charge them *more*. You have the experience to command top dollar for your skill or trade once you reach this point that it takes you less time to complete. Not to mention, your clients get things on a faster turnaround because it takes you less time to complete a job. This is not to say that you shouldn't charge a rush fee if your client demands an extremely tight turnaround time (we'll cover this toward the end of the book).

The major takeaway for this point is that you don't want to shortchange yourself in the long run by charging hourly. Let's consider my example of my first job paying $5 per article which took me an hour. Now, I can write 500 words in about twenty minutes. Does that mean I should only make $1.25? That would be an unsustainable way to make a living and would require me to have many clients to reach my financial goals. Freelancers can charge higher rates when they charge per project because clients have an anticipation of how many hours it should take. They don't need to know that you're proficient and can turn around the project in less time. The truth is that it really isn't any of their business how long it takes you if you're being paid on a per-project basis. As long as you are delivering the completed project on the timetable you both agreed to (or sooner), then you shouldn't have to answer for how long a project takes you. Sometimes, it will take you a little longer than anticipated but the inverse of this is also true. In the end, it usually balances out once you get accustomed to your workflow and speed.

Better Expectations for the Client

BEYOND THE IDEA THAT you may be leaving money on the table by working quickly when a job pays hourly, I think it actually works out in the client's favor to charge them for an entire project instead of your hourly rate. Especially for new freelancers, you might not have a firm grasp on how long something will take you yet. Even if you are doing the same thing you did at your day job, there is a good chance you never timed yourself to see how long it took you to complete a task. You were clocked in and paid for every hour in your cubicle or you were on salary, so it didn't matter down to the minute how long it took you to achieve completion.

The same is not true when you are working for a client on an hourly basis. When you sign up a new client for your services, chances are they are going to want to know how long it will take you to complete the scope of work. This is different than a deadline when you're working on an hourly basis. What they are really asking you is how much the project is going to cost them in the end. Most clients aren't happy to give you an unlimited number of hours to complete their project because they have a budget to stick to, and your hourly wage is the biggest variable in their bottom line.

Freelancers who go way over the hours they agreed to work may face a real challenge. They might have to complete work for no pay in order to comply with the original guidelines. If the client has not altered the scope of work since you started the project and you told them it would take between five and seven hours, you need to wrap it up in five to seven hours. A client who gets hit with an unexpected bill because you worked ten to twelve hours is extremely unlikely to leave you a positive review which lessens your chances of getting a subsequent job on whatever platform you are using. Burn too many bridges this way and your career as a freelancer is doomed before it even starts.

Clients might have an expectation of how long something should take, even if they would never nail you down from the beginning. Make sure you let them know roughly how many hours it would take to complete a job before you sign a contract or accept an offer. If you put in more hours than they expect even if they told you it was fine, it will be an unwelcome surprise that might jeopardize your long-term relationship with them if there was an opportunity for future collaboration.

Some clients don't realize the benefits and security offered to them when they pay a hired freelancer on a per-project basis. I always take a minute early in the negotiation process of contracts to educate them on the benefits to *them* if we can settle on a per-project basis. They are used to the hourly model because this is standard in many industries, but most are eager to switch to a project basis when they realize that it's easier for them to budget. Jobs that are advertised at an hourly rate usually get a quick question in my proposal to ask them if they are open to other payment options. I usually frame it as "Would you be open to negotiating payment on a per-project basis? I find this gives you a better expectation of the cost of the project and eliminates unwanted surprises at the completion." I rarely come across someone who turns me down with this short introduction to the idea. Advocate for yourself, get paid what you deserve, and don't fret about clocking in and out.

More Flexibility in Scheduling

DO YOU WORK A NON-TRADITIONAL schedule? It may not appear totally professional if you do all of your work at 2:00 AM – and if you use a time clock software like that found on Upwork, your client *will* know that you are doing their work in the middle of the night. Part of the reason why you decided to become a freelancer was so you could work when and where you want. You can eliminate questions about your dedication to the project simply by delivering the project on the date it is due without tracking screenshots via time clock software. If you choose to work hourly, you could also do manual time entries to make it look like you worked in the afternoon rather than in the middle of the night. This is just something to consider if you're thinking about moving to an hourly rate for your first few jobs while you figure out what to charge.

How to Charge Per Project

AND NOW, WE HAVE COME to the most important question: how do you charge for a project if you decide to deviate from an hourly pay rate? This is the meatiest question that people have when it comes to pricing their services and I'm not here to give you a one-size-fits-all solution. The hourly rate you calculated in our earlier chapters still comes in handy here because you will need to figure out how long this project will take you. Your calculations might be a bit off when you first start, but you will quickly understand what is required to get the same types of projects done. In these early days, do your best to estimate how long it will take you in hours and then add one to three hours to this figure. If you think it will only take one hour, adding a single additional hour might be sufficient. If it's a longer project, I would add three to four hours to the final cost. Chances are it will take you longer than you think it will, and this covers your cost.

New freelancers hesitate to do this because they realize that every penny counts when they are trying to convince a client to take a risk on hiring them as an unproven worker. Again, this is very similar to getting a one-time job just to gain experience. You could price your services just at your normal hourly rate for your expected number of hours – if it's a one-time gig. You don't want to set the stage that you will work for the bare minimum moving forward, especially if it ends up taking you longer than you think it will. For example, I once took a job writing 1,500-word articles for $50 each for a content management company. Ordinarily, this would take me about an hour but these particular articles took me two hours to complete. Even as a seasoned freelancer, I made a miscalculation on how long it took me to come up with a finished project. I quickly had to pivot because I wasn't making enough to cover my time. I went against my better judgment, quoted a price too low for the market, and ended up paying for it. I should have banked on an extra hour or two which would have been reasonable for the research required to write these highly specific and detailed articles.

If you bid on a recurring project and realize you didn't charge enough, you will be faced with two real options. For the agreed-upon work, you might need to simply put your head down and do the work as discussed. It isn't up to the client to compensate you for time you didn't plan to spend on their project. When you know better, you can do better and quote more realistic prices to clients, but this takes quite a bit of practice. After the agreed-upon work is completed, you can propose two options to the client: either you need to raise your rates or you need to stop your work together. This is painful if you had been hoping for them to be recurring clients and you were banking on that income. Not everyone will be happy with a rate increase unless you can prove your services are worth it and you can seriously deliver on your promises.

You may also choose to just continue with the work – for a time. There is an art to charging more for your services, and you may simply not be there yet. New freelancers often do work that they aren't compensated for simply to gain experience on the platform or even with a whole new skill. If you have never written a blog post or managed a social media campaign before, this might not be the time to think about charging top dollar for a service you can't necessarily deliver. Take the work as it comes and use it to build out your portfolio, gain experience, get faster, and ultimately delight your clients. After you have significant growth in these skill areas, you might be able to justify charging more. This means you'll need to stick with it for longer than just one or two articles, a single Facebook ad campaign, or a flyer design. When they see your growth as a freelancer and note the benefit of having you on their team, it is time to increase your rates.

There is another piece of the puzzle to consider when quoting a large job. It will take up a good chunk of your time and will keep you from needing to apply to other jobs for a set period of time while the project is ongoing. Especially if it is something you will be working on for months, you might decide to offer a discount on the entire project. While the specific discount you give will depend on the circumstances (we'll dive into this later), it can be a good way to secure steady work that is worth its weight in gold. If you would ordinarily charge $1,500 for the job, then a quote at $1,250 might be perfectly reasonable. It might place you on the lower side of the average, but you have guaranteed work until the project comes to completion. Plus, your rates will be kept in mind when the client needs future work in the same vein and you may end up getting a repeat client just because you offered fair rates and a discount for services.

The amount you charge is only half of the battle when it comes to setting your rates. No matter how much (or how little) you charge, clients will inevitably have questions about how you settled on a rate. You need to learn how to convey your prices with confidence and without guilt. After all, you are providing a service that matters to someone and can have a major impact on their business and bottom line. The next chapter will show you how to take the figure you land on and share it with your clients without guilt.

Communicating Price without Guilt

Inevitably, you will come across a client who will question your rates even if they're in line with the rest of the marketplace. In a world where we negotiate and haggle over the price of cars and cable bills, everyone is seeking out a discount. There are times when you can afford to offer a small discount to a prospective client, but it should *not* be your default whenever you submit a proposal for a job well suited to your skills. Instead, you should price your services fairly for your level of experience, the turnaround time, and the amount of time it will take you to bring the job to a satisfactory completion for both you and the client. If you price your services fairly from the outset, there is no need to think about offering a discount.

Communicate your prices clearly and without guilt to save yourself a lot of heartache down the road. Offering a discount for every service and every project will quickly shortchange and burn you out on the freelancing lifestyle. Confidence in your pricing comes with time, and there is no doubt that you will feel uncomfortable charging people for your services at the beginning of your career. The good news is that communicating prices clearly and without guilt requires just a few mindset shifts. These mindset shifts will help you when someone calls your quote into question – without having to offer them a better deal than you already have.

This is a Business

THE FIRST MINDSET SHIFT that you absolutely must make before you even quote the very first job is that this is a business. A business is an enterprise with the sole purpose of generating revenue for the business owner and his or her employees. Even if you are the only employee in your business, you still deserve to make a living by providing skills and goods to the marketplace. You would never go to Target or Walmart and haggle with the cashier over the price of a dozen eggs or a new sweater. You need to treat your business here with the same respect as a retail location. The price you quote *is* the price of the service – no questions asked.

Of course, you have already walked through the steps to pricing your services and the final numbers aren't arbitrary. While you never have to justify your pricing to a client, it helps you to know how and why you value a project at a certain rate. When a customer calls your pricing into question, you can relay the calculations to them in a respectful way. You don't have to share with them the number of sick days you plan to take a year or your hourly rate (if you're pricing per project). However, you can give them some perspective on how much work is going to go into any given project and the experience that you bring to the table.

Think of it this way: you head to the car dealership and you want to order a new car. The salesperson is going to ask you whether you want leather seats, a remote starter, extra cupholders, or an upgraded sound system. For each item that you add, there is a price associated with it. If you want the item, you pay the fee and don't ask too many questions about it. The salesperson isn't making this personal: there are set rates for each item you add to your new vehicle. Likewise, a freelancing service isn't personal. It is a business just as much as a car dealership. When a client wants the services or outcome you offer, they have to pay the price.

This is why it is so crucial to do the heavy lifting of calculating your rates before you even start to bid on projects on a freelancing platform of your choosing. For some people, it might even make sense for them to narrow down what they offer to a few distinct packages. For example, a freelance writer might come up with a package of four 500-word blog posts, four 1,000-word blog posts, or a technical paper of a certain length. You can settle on a price for those services in advance and share them with your client via a neat and clean flyer. They can then pick and choose from the services offered and see what best aligns with their budget in order to work with you. This flyer doesn't have to be overly complex, requiring the input of a graphic designer. A simple PDF file is sufficient. The benefit is it makes you look more professional and polished, which makes your clients less likely to treat this as anything other than a bona fide business.

Freelancing is just as much a business as any other service: a dry cleaner, an advertising agency, a graphic design firm, or a content creation service. Most people wouldn't think of going to a brick-and-mortar location and offering someone less than the going rate. Take this philosophy into your freelancing and remember this business is no different. When you embrace it as a business over a hobby, you have better odds of getting the prices required to really make a go of launching a freelance business.

Understand Your Value

THIS MINDSET SHIFT might take a little while for you to feel established in your career but try to keep it in mind even at the very beginning. Your services provide real value to clients, regardless of what field you work in. I want you to take a moment and write down exactly what a client gains from their interaction with you. Think about your most recent proposal: what were you *really* providing for your clients? It might have been a piece of content for their blog, but it's more than that. Instead, think of it as providing content that encourages engagement from their audience and leads to a five percent increase in paying customers. Designing a logo? Not anymore; you're improving brand identity and helping businesses attract more of their ideal customers.

Have you noticed the common thread here? Your service goes beyond just the deliverable you provide to a client at the conclusion of your contract. Every service you provide serves to increase a client's bottom line when done successfully. Otherwise, why would they pay for that service? People are making money from the services that you provide in one way or another, even if it seems indirect to you at the outset. Businesses would never invest in your services if they thought there was going to be no return on their investment. You are providing an excellent value for them and you deserve a cut of the profits of what they're going to make from what you give to them.

Consider the monetary gain of your services and realize your services could be the sort of investment a client needs to take their business to the very next level. You may be charging them $50 or $500, but what is their return on the investment going to be? If you do your job right, they might see a tenfold increase or more. Even more modest gains are still worth taking another look at. It might be hard for you to quantify the gains for the business because you aren't managing their books, but you can rest assured that *every* service a freelancer provides can move the needle forward for the business. From marketing materials to content management and branding design to translation services, businesses are gaining financially from your services. Value yourself and claim your piece of the pie for the financial gain of these companies. This is *not* taking advantage of them. It is simply getting what is due to you for the contribution of your services.

Think about this in a real-world context: the initial marketing director at Mint Mobile didn't value his services the same way Mint Mobile did. They offered him a six-figure salary but he thought he was too young and too inexperienced to provide the value that they were looking for. Still, he accepted the job (he would have been crazy not to!). When they sold the company later on down the road, the valuation was substantially more than his six-figure salary. He positioned Mint as a leader in the telecommunications industry and someone was willing to pay big bucks to buy the business he helped build. He undervalued his contribution and was surprised to see just what he was able to do at the end of the day. His value exceeded his salary.

If you aren't sure what your service provides to a business at the end of the day, you may need to revisit what you're doing prior to evaluating how much you charge. Your clients should be gaining real value from whatever you have to offer, so it makes sense that you would need to charge based on that final outcome. Be confident in what you can help them achieve, share those experiences and successes with them, and charge what you are worth.

Discuss Rates Openly

HOW CAN YOU COMMUNICATE your rates without feeling guilt over the number is in black and white at the end of the day? The best thing you can do is be open and honest about your rates in every conversation with your prospective client. If you spend a lot of time dodging the question of what you will charge for a given service, you give off the vibe you are uncomfortable charging for what you have on offer. The result? Clients feel like they can pay you less because they sense you aren't confident in yourself, your skills, or your services. They need to know the exact value that you provide them – and you should start this conversation as early as possible.

Start conversations about money and rates early and often during the initial negotiation of the scope of work the client needs to complete. For many freelancers, this is easy enough. If you're using Upwork, there is a line item in your proposal that asks for your rate for the job. While clients can come back to you to haggle over the rates, they have some idea of what you're going to charge them before they even open up the conversation with you. If your rates are too high for what they are looking for, they simply don't have to contact you and can easily go with another freelancer who has the ability to charge less (or maybe they haven't done the hard work you've been doing in this book).

If you leave your discussion of pricing to the very end of your conversation about the scope of work, you might find you have wasted a lot of time with the back and forth. They might think you are priced too high, even though they understand the value you provide. At this point, you may feel the sunk cost of your time in the back and forth about their expectations and deliverables. In fact, you might feel so invested in their project that you're willing to take the lower rates they are willing to offer you instead of placing value on yourself and your talents. Freelancers need to be open about their rates and set the expectation that they will need to be paid fairly for their work from the very beginning. It helps everyone avoid nasty pricing surprises that can leave a bitter taste in the mouth of your client which can lead to bad reviews and a discontinuation of your contract.

Saving Clients Money

YOU SHOULD ALSO THINK about all of the ways you are actually saving your clients money, which is an important component of your pricing. Think about what they would have to pay a full-time worker who provides the same services you are offering them. Between salary, benefits, and taxes, they will be thousands of dollars in the hole without even thinking about the onboarding process and necessary training to get the job done right. Freelancers can be hired for their specialized skills and can be paid for only what they deliver. There is no need to worry about how a client can keep a full-time (or even a part-time) worker busy day in and day out.

Freelancers only need to be paid for the hours or work they put in, and there is no need to keep them on a retainer for a set number of hours if it isn't what the role calls for. Plus, clients don't need to provide health insurance and other benefits. Even employer payroll taxes are avoided when bringing a freelancer on board. This means clients can usually afford to pay a little more for a freelancer instead of a full-time worker. If you calculated you need to charge more for your service than you made at your last day job, that doesn't mean it isn't feasible. Many clients are more than willing to pay a little more for the convenience of having a freelancer and the way they can save money. Paying a freelancer is a straightforward transaction: the rates you both agree on are the only money that has to change hands and they have no need for financial heavy lifting in their accounting department when payroll is due.

Becoming confident in what you charge is an art that comes with time. Oftentimes, it is more of a mindset shift than a need to alter your rates. You need to be confident in what you charge, the value you provide, and the ways that you are actually saving a client money. Be open about your rates from the beginning of your conversation and remember this is a business. Combine them all together and you have the ability to price your services with confidence and can communicate that to your clients without guilt. If you decide to offer a discount, make sure you do so with intention and a strategic mindset. Let's take a look at when you might lower your rates for a client.

Discounts

Clients will eventually ask you for a discount on your going rates, and their questions may not be malicious toward you or your growing business. Many people feel like they have to offer a lower rate in order to get the best deal on a service. So many things in our lives are negotiable these days that it just makes sense they may try to apply this philosophy to your rates. Sometimes, clients do not offer lower rates because they can't afford your services. Instead, they are simply trying to cut their bottom line as much as possible. Clients aren't concerned about *your* bottom line, so you must learn to prioritize your pricing.

Too many freelancers give into the expectation they will hand out discounts and the initial price quoted is never the bottom line; clients have come to expect that there will be a discount. What can you do to combat this mentality that your rates aren't definitive? Here are some things to consider when facing a client who wants a better price than what you have on offer.

Strategic Price Discounts

THE FIRST THING TO clarify is that there may indeed be a time to hand out price discounts, but that is something that should be handled strategically with lots of thought into what you can offer. Often, I recommend that freelancers offer a discount to the first few clients they onboard or for a specific time period when they are getting their fledgling business off the ground. If you have a client who needs something that will take you just a few hours and will then be over, you could offer a lower rate for this short and sweet job in exchange for a positive review which lends you credibility for a higher-paying position.

Alternatively, you may decide to offer a lower price for a set period of time if you mostly take on recurring clients. A recurring client is one you will work with long-term such as on social media marketing or content management. There is no clear end date on the work you will do with this client, and you may not want to work at this lower rate for an extended period. To this end, you can charge a lower introductory rate for the first few weeks or months of your contract with them. Always be clear about your rates from the outset, including sharing your introductory rate and the rate you will charge once that initial period ends. Communicate it without guilt and don't give your client room to negotiate the price you decided upon once the introductory period ends. If you suspect a client will not be willing to pay your higher rate long-term, you may choose not to work with them or to take their positive review and move on to the next client.

Before you offer a discount to a client just because they ask, I want you to really evaluate the value you are providing them with like you did in the last chapter. Communicate what you will be providing them with for the rates you set, being sure not to sell yourself short. It can be tempting to take every job that comes your way – especially in the beginning. But I want you to think about what this will ultimately cost you in the long run. Picture what your salary would be if you worked only at the going rate you calculated. Now, picture what salary you will earn if you work at these new discounted rates. Chances are there is a substantial difference between these two figures.

Can you afford to work for this lower rate, pay your bills, and get your business off the ground?

Now, I want you to think about what it means to take on a lower-paying position. Every hour you spend on this project, valued well below your average rate, is one less hour you can spend on a higher-paying project. You are literally losing money and missing out on clients who would be happy to pay your rates because they understand the inherent value of working with a freelancer. There is a distinct advantage for clients who don't want to hire full-time employees. It might sound expensive to hire someone off the bat, but if you can relate how much they are really going to *save* by hiring you, they are going to be more willing to part with their hard-earned cash.

When You Don't Want to Discount Your Services

STRATEGIC DISCOUNTS are great for branching into a new field where you might need to build up your skills or your reputation. However, there will come a time when you need to consider whether a discount is really the right move for your business. That is how I want you to think about this: as a business that needs to pay your bills and cover your cost of living. Discounts are not going to be the right answer forever, so you need to get confident in pricing your services appropriately from the start. This doesn't mean you should inflate your quotes so you have room to offer a discount to your clients when they inevitably ask. An added fee onto your base rate might actually push you out of the range of what a client can pay and make you a less competitive option even if you are the best freelancer for the job. Instead, you should price them competitively from the start, and be clear you don't offer discounts on services rendered.

One way you can demonstrate that your prices are fair and reasonable for the market is to break them down for your client. If you know how many hours a project should take you, then you can create a black-and-white breakdown of exactly where their money is going. You may consider making a template for the services you offer most frequently. With this already in place, all you have to do is substitute the number of hours spent in each area. For example, we'll look at how I might break down the project of writing a blog post for a client into three phases: research, writing, and editing. I will spend one hour researching, two hours writing, and thirty minutes editing. This shows my client where their money is going and exactly what they are paying for each service.

It also allows them to see areas where they can trim expenses if they choose to do so. Our above example might trim expenses by providing the research or a detailed outline of the blog they want to be written. They might decide to edit it in-house and save me thirty minutes of editing. I can still work in my zone of genius with writing the post, but they might be able to shave off an hour or an hour and a half of my work by taking the burden on themselves. When the bottom line is the most important consideration for them, these shortcuts are a great opportunity for you to land a job that is little work for you and pays fairly based on your going rates. I would recommend using a program like Google Sheets to create this form so that it calculates all of your sums automatically for you, ensuring a math error won't shortchange you at the end of the day.

Offering a discount simply because someone asks for it devalues what you are offering in the marketplace. You have the right to charge fairly for the services you provide, and I want you to really think about what a discount costs you in word of mouth. Let's say that you offer one CEO a discounted rate on their logo and branding design because they ask for it. You complete the work and feel miserable because you didn't make enough to cover your costs or pay your bills. Now, it might be okay to do this just once to gain more business. But what happens when that CEO tells someone else where they got their branding done and what a steep discount they received for that service? Chances are you will have others lining up at your door to get in on the action. Nobody wants to pay full price for your services because they already have the expectation it isn't worth what they might be charged full price.

At this point, you have two clear options: you can continue to extend the discount to other CEOs who come to you via word-of-mouth advertising or you can charge higher rates and deal with the pushback you are likely to get. Neither of these options is ideal. In one, you work for rates that are too low to sustain your business. On the other hand, it damages your reputation. The best way to avoid this scenario is to charge what you want to charge from the outset, as long as you know your rates are in line with the market and commensurate with your experience.

This is not to say that you can *never* increase your rates. Eventually, you might encounter a time when you need to raise your rates and will have to deal with the pushback that comes with a rate hike (more on this in a later chapter). However, an immediate price change when a contract concludes can feel like a bait-and-switch tactic, especially if you knew this project was going to be ongoing when you added it to your docket.

Can You Afford to Work for Less?

THERE WILL ALWAYS BE clients who want to haggle with you, nickeling and diming you into offering them your rock-bottom rates. In other words, there will always be someone who wants to pay you less than you deserve. I think most businesses that are perceived as negotiable will encounter a few of these clients at some point over the course of their careers. Even retail locations sometimes face the negotiation process. I used to work in home remodeling and we frequently had people ask for discounts on flooring and installation. The final price was never the "final" price in their minds, and this is often the case for freelancers as well.

I want you to really take a minute to think about the rates you set at the beginning of this book. Chances are they seem reasonable to you after breaking down what you need to do to make an honest living with your services, to cover your taxes, and to pay for your overhead. Now, you have a number in mind of what you need to make per hour to keep a roof over your head and food on your table. Let's say that the number you settled on was $40 per hour. Someone will always come along and offer you a lesser number: let's call it $10 per hour. This sounds like a substantial discount, but I assure you that you will eventually come across a client who has no respect for your pricing, services, or quality. You could take this lower fee if you're determined to get a few jobs under your belt in the very beginning, which can be a strategic decision on your part. However, it doesn't make for a sustainable business model moving forward.

You might feel that nagging guilt in the back of your mind telling you that you need to offer a less expensive service, even after you have the first few jobs under your belt. After all, this is your passion and it feels more like a hobby to you than a career. A good freelancer wants to give their very best to every project and might feel like they're charging above fair market value if they encounter tire kickers at every stage of their career. Now, you *could* work for $10 per hour because that is what your prospective client is willing to pay. Just because they can afford to pay you $10 per hour doesn't mean that *you* can afford to work for $10 per hour. While your business is client-centric, this doesn't mean you need to cater to every client who comes along offering you well below the average rate for your services. Think about what you can afford to work for (and chances are it isn't anything less than you discovered in the earlier chapters). Don't compromise on your rates just because someone else feels you should have to.

Of course, discounts are really just the tip of the iceberg. You will eventually be faced with requests not just for a discount but for free work altogether. How do you handle these requests and how can you head them off from the very beginning? The next chapter dives into how you can handle these requests with grace without compromising your integrity or your profit.

Free Work

I wish I could tell you I never had anyone devalue my work by asking if I could work for free. I have no idea why, but some clients feel entitled to ask freelancers to work for nothing with no real intention of ever transitioning into being a paid client. Over the years, I faced numerous scenarios where a client asked me to provide them with a blog post free of charge, to ensure that we were a good fit for one another. I fell for this scam early in my career, working hard on a test piece so that I would be considered for the long-term position only to be ghosted when all was wrapped up. Too many times, I never heard from those clients again. They got their free content (likely from several freelancers) and they had no need to pay for services.

The truth is I know it can be tempting to jump on every opportunity coming your way when you leave your day job and start freelancing full-time. Any chance to work should be taken seriously because it can lead to a paid contract that puts food on the table. Unfortunately, the type of clients who ask you to work for free aren't usually the type to become paying clients. If they do become paying clients, chances are it will be well below your usual rate because they will be sure to ask for a discount. After all, you already did work for free so your services must not be valued at the figures you decided in advance. Sound familiar?

Here are a couple of ways you can handle requests for free work.

Create a Portfolio

ONE WAY YOU CAN HEAD off requests for free work to determine if you are a good fit for a position is to develop a portfolio of the best examples of the services you offer. Unless you are under a non-disclosure agreement (NDA), you may be able to use examples of work you completed at your day job to flesh out a robust portfolio. Some sites allow you to upload a unique portfolio to your profile, whether that means just a handful of samples or something more extensive.

I encourage you to spend some time thinking about what your bread-and-butter services are going to be at the start of your freelance career so you can create a portfolio showcasing those skills. Maybe you have heard the old adage there are riches in niches. This is applicable to your freelancing career as well. Be as specific as you can be about who you will serve and what you will offer so your portfolio leaves no question that you can deliver on your promises. How specific should you be in the beginning? I will give an example from my own career: I write on topics such as entrepreneurship, personal finance, and mental health. I write both short-form and long-form content (think blogs versus books). This might seem like I'm pigeonholing myself into a very narrow niche, but I promise you I have found an abundance of work by narrowing down my field of expertise.

This also allows me to tailor my portfolio to those different areas. I have examples of short blogs, essays, and even chapters from books that serve as a foundation for what services I offer. When someone asks if I can complete a short blog article for them free of charge, I tell them no (in a nice way). I might say something like, "I'm really sorry not to be able to work for free, but here is an example of a blog article I wrote for another client in this same niche to give you an idea of my style and writing ability." Most people realize how unreasonable it is to expect anyone to work without pay – freelancer or not. This puts their request in perspective and most will happily accept a specific piece of content that will give them the confidence they need to feel that they are going to receive the service that they pay for.

What do you do if you have no previous examples because you are branching into a new field or you can't use examples from your day job because they were a collaborative effort or you are bound by an NDA? Fear not, it is still possible to build a portfolio of samples you can refer a client to if you want to avoid this phenomenon of working for free. Instead, you can work for free (for yourself) once and then use those examples over and over again in your portfolio. There are lots of different ways to approach building up a portfolio when you have no client work to speak of.

First, you can browse job boards for descriptions that sound like your ideal position and then create an item based on the targets they want you to hit. For example, you might design a social media campaign for a dentist's office or write a short white paper about cryptocurrency. If you have a hard time finding active job descriptions that would be ideal for you or they lack the details that would allow you to create a sample piece of content for them, you can make them up. Nobody has to know the pieces you create weren't for actual client work – and you shouldn't volunteer this information to them either. Suppose you want to write on political issues or want to design logos. You can make up a client and write a sample piece on the presidential candidates in the next election. Make up fifteen companies and design a logo for each one, keeping only the very best in your portfolio.

Now, you have a response when someone asks you for a trial piece. It may not be tailored completely to their prospective job, but it should be close enough to give them an idea of your abilities. A client who refuses to use their imagination to see how you can stretch and expand to complete their job based on a similar profile may not be a good fit for you. This should be a huge red flag they are going to continuously ask you for free work and discounts which doesn't set the stage for a successful working relationship moving forward. If they are insistent that you give them free work, it might be better to walk away than to cater to unreasonable demands.

Spend No More than 15 Minutes

MAYBE YOU ARE THINKING about branching out into a new area but you haven't had time to design a portfolio of example pieces yet. Still, you found a job description that sounds like the ideal position for you. It pays your average rates and promises ongoing work for the right freelancer. If they ask you for free work, it might be okay to give them a small taste of what you can do in order to cinch the deal. Plus, this free work could contribute to your portfolio moving forward with a little more work and polishing. When this exact scenario presents itself to you, then you may want to think about offering a free trial period – if you can complete something in fifteen minutes or less.

No, you won't be able to write a 1,000-word article in less than fifteen minutes – and clients shouldn't expect this from you when it comes to giving free work. It might mean that you can only write a paragraph or two, but make them the best paragraphs you absolutely can. This doesn't mean you should skip proofreading and polishing them in an effort to save time or cut corners. On the other hand, visual artists might be able to provide rough sketches of their ideas for the project and spend just a few minutes showing their scope and abilities. When the client wants something more refined, then they need to pay for your services.

In this situation, I might offer a discount to someone who genuinely wants to take a chance on a freelancer at the start of their career. I might cut my rate by 25 to 50 percent for this *first piece only*. The result is that I get a piece I can add to my portfolio, they get a much clearer idea of what I can offer them and the value I'm providing, and I still get to cover some of my time costs for the project. The catch here is that you have to be extremely clear about what your rates are after this initial test piece. Unfortunately, you will likely find that some clients are only out to get what they can for a free or reduced price. You may deliver the finished project for this initial piece and then never hear from them again. I've certainly experienced my fair share of ghost clients who got all they could at my discounted rate and then left.

Alternatively, they use this discounted rate as a means to nickel and dime me, demanding more services or edits at no cost to them. For clients who pay my full rate, I'm more than happy to offer a round of editing or revision, if necessary, at no additional charge. I offer this because I'm mostly confident I provide what a client wants from the start, due in part to the fact I've been doing this for more than twelve years. I know what questions to ask and how to get the details I need to meet expectations on every project. However, I may not be as willing to provide this for free if I'm only getting paid half of my usual rate. I simply can't sink that much time into something that doesn't pay enough to cover my overhead costs or my salary or contribute in a meaningful way to my bottom line.

Communicate Boundaries

DECIDING WHETHER YOU will work for free is ultimately a personal decision you will have to make. There are no right or wrong answers at the start of your career, though I would certainly caution you away from providing this as your portfolio and reputation grow. The best thing you can do for yourself and your business is to communicate clear boundaries with your client before the project commences. If you are going to provide them with free work, be extremely clear about exactly what you will provide them with at no cost to them. In other words, don't allow them to think they are going to get a polished project from start to finish at no cost. You might be willing to write a couple of paragraphs to demonstrate your knowledge in the field or to assemble some font choices for a flyer design, but you won't do the whole project for free, especially if there is no clear chance for recurring work.

Clients are going to want to see what they can get for free, so stand your ground on the value you provide to them. They need to respect your time and talent because you are a professional even if you do work in your pajamas from the comfort of your couch. You may not *feel* like an expert in these early days, but I promise you it will come with time. Every freelancer struggles with imposter syndrome at some point, this feeling that they aren't worth the rates that they want to charge for a service rendered. Don't allow imposter syndrome to convince you to supply clients with free or discounted work just because you aren't sure if anything you do is worth the price you want to charge. If you can set boundaries in place early and often, you will become much more confident when it comes to charging for your services.

Some clients are going to be okay asking you for free work or trial pieces to prove your talent, but this is not the only unreasonable request you are likely to face from clients. Some of them neglect to plan ahead for their projects and need things on a shorter timetable. It means you might need to drop everything to help them out of a bind that they put themselves in – and that comes at a price. The next chapter will help you figure out how to pass along that price to your clients so you can afford to neglect other work and assist them.

One of my favorite sayings is that a lack of planning on your part doesn't constitute an emergency on my part. This is so applicable to the life of a freelancer because clients often find that they didn't plan for enough time to get their project done by their deadline. As a result, they think that whoever they hire should let go of all their other projects and prioritize their project first and foremost. You could make a decent living doing nothing but completing projects for clients who fail to recognize time constraints on their existing team. In fact, a client might do this so regularly that you can come to expect them as a recurring client every so often when their full-time team can't get to the influx associated with a new project.

Of course, you likely have a docket of paying clients right now who need updates on their progress too. It might not be feasible for you to quit everything else you're doing in order to get a different project done on a crunched timeline. You will need to consider how this will work from a logistical point of view before you agree to a rush job. First, you will need to think about whether you have the time to get this job done in a realistic window. With all of the other projects in the lineup, is it reasonable to knock out a large project in a week or two without compromising on the deadlines of your other projects? Delaying other clients in an effort to clear your docket for a client may not be feasible because other clients have deadlines too – and they're counting on you to meet them as agreed upon. Pushing back their deadline might result in a negative review which can hurt more than the positive review that might come out of helping a client out of a bind.

The next thing you might want to consider is whether this is a past client. They might get more priority treatment if they have worked with you in the past, you already know their standards and guidelines, and they have provided prompt payment. A client who doesn't usually request rush jobs but has a deadline coming up they just can't meet without your help might garner a little bit of sympathy from you as their freelancer. If you can swing it in your schedule, you may decide to work a little extra this week or this month in order to meet their deadline. They will likely value you more for helping them out of a bind and will keep you in mind for any future projects they need – maybe well in advance of their deadline next time.

Of course, you might also consider whether this is going to be an ongoing project. Will they always have work for you, delivered at the last minute with minimal turnaround time allotted? Some freelancers don't mind working under the pressure of tight deadlines while others may thrive with a longer lead time that allows them to juggle all of their responsibilities and permits them to work the flexible schedule that drew them into freelancing in the first place. The good news is if you can swing these last-minute projects, you might find you have a loyal client for life – and it may be financially beneficial for you as well. That's right; you can charge more for a rush job than you do one completed on a more leisurely timeline. We'll look at how you can up your fees for rush jobs in the next section.

Charging for Rush Jobs

THIS SECTION MAY NOT give you a concrete answer on how much you should charge for a rush job, but it should give you some ideas and guidelines for charging appropriately. You should never drop everything for a client who assigns you work at the last minute. Just because they didn't plan ahead doesn't mean you need to treat their problem as an emergency. This is not about the beloved client who has never asked for this before who had something pop up last minute and thought of you. If this is your situation, you may consider waiving a rush job fee if they are a spectacular client who has a history of being generous with deadlines (and pay). An unknown client, even a recurring one, should warrant an extra fee for their last-minute, spur-of-the-moment gig.

There are a couple of ways you could handle a rush fee on your projects. The first is to up your hourly rate in accordance with the deadline given. For example, you may add a 50 percent markup to your hourly rate for a project with a turnaround time of a week or less. This is perhaps the most straightforward way to rearrange your pricing because it accounts for each and every hour you spend working on their project, to the detriment of your other work. A 50 percent increase may seem steep, but I would argue that this should be the standard when you are an experienced worker who has the exact skill set a client needs and who can work with an unreasonable deadline for a major project. Even a less seasoned freelancer should charge at least 25 to 30 percent more per hour for a project that will consume your every waking moment for the next week or so.

What if their project isn't due in a week or less, giving you a little more time to work around it with your other projects? You could always lessen the markup on your hourly rate because you won't necessarily have to abandon all of your other projects which could put you behind elsewhere on your schedule of projects. A tight timeline should still warrant a rush fee, but you can be a little more lenient if you have a few weeks to turn it around and still work on other client projects. In this case, I would recommend a 25 percent increase hourly for experienced freelancers and at least a 10 to 15 percent increase for new freelancers who are still feeling out where their rates should be set.

At this point, you might be wondering exactly what kind of turnaround time justifies a rush fee. The answer is a little less clear; it depends on exactly which industry you work in because one idea of a tight deadline for a writer might not be the same for a translator. A web designer might have a different idea of a tight turnaround time than both of those categories. A good rule of thumb is to figure out what your usual deadline would be for this type of project. Maybe a turnaround time of one week would be ideal for you if you're writing something short like brochure copy. In this situation, a 48-hour turnaround time might warrant a rush job fee. On the other hand, a website designer might need a full month to complete a website to their standards. A one-week turnaround time would definitely warrant a rush fee because they would have to compress four weeks of time into just one.

Think about what your usual turnaround time would be and then compare. Any job that would significantly alter your delivery would warrant the higher rush job fee while a job that only crunches your deadlines a little bit might get a smaller rush fee. In other words, you should think about how inconvenient this new project is going to be for you to complete and price your services accordingly. Explain to clients that you will have to drop other work to intensively focus on their current project which will warrant an increase in your fees for this priority service. You might get some pushback on these increased rates, especially if you never charged them in the past. This type of increase in your rates should help cover the cost of work you will be losing out on in other areas. The idea isn't to be vindictive against your clients but to make up for what you will not be able to complete in the same timeframe.

Not all freelancers charge hourly, though. Project-based rates should still have an increase in price for rush jobs, but you can do this a couple of different ways. The most straightforward way to move a project along is to charge a flat fee to be bumped to the top of the queue. You might charge a flat $200 or $250 per project, but the rate that makes the most sense depends on your area of expertise and the going rate for your services. Obviously, you would not charge a $200 rush fee for a project that should only total $50 on a regular basis. If all of your contracts are roughly the same price because you are doing roughly the same job all the time, then figuring out a rush fee that makes sense for your industry might be a little easier. This is a one-time fee you levy with any client who needs this type of priority service. It's easy for your client to understand the breakdown of costs and what to expect when they get their final bill at the end of the project.

Some freelancers will have a harder time figuring out what type of rush fee to charge due to fluctuating contracts. One client might need $1,000 worth of work while another only nets you about $200. Obviously, you don't want to charge the same rush fee for both projects. Your larger client would get the better deal, which may make them inclined to repeatedly put you in a position to abandon your other projects and give them priority. It doesn't teach them to plan ahead because the cost of waiting until the last minute is so minute. Much like an hourly rush fee, you can tally up the number of hours you think you will spend on their project at your hourly rate (which is ideally how you priced their package of services to begin with). Figure out what percentage markup you want to charge on that hourly rate and the number of hours you will have to work on a compressed timeline, and then add that amount to the final project cost.

Much like pricing your services, there are no hard and fast rules for clients who expect you to work solely on their project for a given time. The important thing here is that you don't neglect your other client work just to get this done on time. Your other clients have just as much of a right to your time as this last-minute client does. If you have already made promises to have something turned around by a given date, your client is counting on you to follow through. Failure to deliver on this promise could cost you a long-term client who would have been otherwise satisfied to give you excellent work time and again. It could result in a negative review because reliability is one of the core components of any rating system for a freelancer. Deliver consistent results on time if you want to maintain a successful career in this field. Rush jobs are nice, especially if you want a little bit of a pay increase and don't mind working longer hours on a short-term basis. However, you absolutely must make sure you have time to get everything done. Don't overestimate how many hours you can work in a week which will lead to burnout and poor work performance for all of your clients.

By this point, you should have a solid grasp on when and how to charge for your services under every circumstance. However, there is more to pricing your services and setting rates than just the bottom-line number. You need to know how to close a deal with confidence which means you need to get comfortable talking about the facts and figures with your clients. We are always told that discussing money isn't a polite topic, but this isn't the time to shy away from the discomfort. In the next chapter, we will talk about

how to close a deal without second-guessing yourself or selling
yourself short.

Closing a Deal with Confidence

O nce you have a grasp on what you should charge and when you should charge more, it's important to figure out how to close the deal with confidence, ensuring you get every penny of what you are owed for the work you do. You don't want a client to say you were unclear with your rates or have them shortchange you when the final project is delivered. Signing a contract is a clear way to ensure that all parties are on the same page when it comes to the scope of work. Setting up a contract is a topic for book four in this series, but we will go over some of the basic tenets of it in this book to help you move forward with getting paid by your first few clients.

Discuss Your Rates Openly

THE FIRST AND MOST important thing you can do when hammering out the finer details of a project is to be clear on your rates. Freelancers who are paid hourly need to be crystal clear on what they charge for each aspect of the job. Some will be paid the same rate, no matter what work they do. Others may have a higher rate for more technical aspects and a lower rate for less intensive services like proofreading and editing. Be clear on what you charge for each service, when you will invoice for services (a set day per week, at the end of a project, etc.), and how many hours you estimate each part of the process is going to take.

It is always a good idea to provide your client with an estimate for your work so there are no unreasonable expectations about what you will complete for a given price. You can create an estimate on your own using Google Sheets or Docs, saving it as a PDF that can easily be shared with others. You may also choose to use platforms like Upwork that allow you to detail every aspect of the project for your clients. You can set up individual milestones that make it clear what the deliverable is at each stage of the project and what the pay is for each phase. These details can be worked into the contract and require approval from both parties before they can be modified.

A milestone created this way also offers some financial security, as most clients will fund a milestone in advance of the work being completed. Then, you can submit the work for every step of the process. Even if your client never gets back to you, Upwork releases the payment fourteen days after submission if it hasn't been approved or disputed by the client. This is the most clarifying way to close your contract with confidence. Everyone knows exactly what you will charge and what they can expect from you in terms of timeline and deliverables.

This explanation of clarity is particularly important when it comes to freelancing for a set rate per project. You need to let a client know exactly what is included in this flat-rate fee or they may start trying to convince you to do "small" things for them for free because you are under contract with them already. Inevitably, these small things usually eat up a significant chunk of time – time that you aren't being paid for and which sets you up for a client to continue asking for free services over and over again. If you need some help telling a client you can't do work for free, be sure to revisit the earlier chapter on free work or trial work.

It can be as simple as saying: "Yes, I would love to help you with that new aspect of your project. It will be $50 more than initially discussed for this add-on service." The point here is to be crystal clear about what is considered outside of the scope of the initially agreed-upon job and how much additional it will cost. Notice that I affirmed the client's request with a yes, pointing out that I'm more than happy to work on something larger for them. My eagerness to communicate with them and to work with them takes precedence over the price, though both are critical parts of the negotiation.

Framing your price increase should always start with the value that you offer to the client and an acknowledgment that what they want is outside the context of the original project. It should be clear exactly *why* you are charging them more for this service. When you receive some pushback on your new rates, you can offer a detailed breakdown as you did in an earlier exercise about pricing your services with confidence. Alternatively, you can tell them that you're happy to keep the project to its original scope and would completely understand if they needed to hire another freelancer in order to complete the additional work. Be honest about what you can and cannot complete within the timeframe. It might hurt to turn down extra work at first. But if you find that you simply can't deliver, it might be better than stressing yourself out over it and putting your mental and physical health in jeopardy.

Don't Second Guess Yourself

MANY CLIENTS ARE NOW interested in meeting with prospective freelancers via video chats or phone calls to ensure that the freelancer is legitimate. With the influx of freelancers to the marketplace, many are not hard workers, may not speak the desired language fluently, and may be difficult to pin down when it comes to price or timeline. It is a lot harder to fake a phone call than it is to send an email that you drafted using ChatGPT or other AI software. For many people, this interview process is the most stressful part of securing a new contract because being on camera with a new client is nerve-wracking – even for seasoned freelancers, who may not be extroverted. After all, there is a reason you are choosing to work from home.

This means you need to maintain professional boundaries when pricing your service and communicating with a potential client. Some freelancers may have a hard time stating their price and dealing with the uncomfortable silence that ensues. Your conversation may follow the same trajectory each and every time: "Usually, I charge $40 per hour for editing a novel." Silence from your client. "But I could do it for $25." Does this sound familiar? Many people have a hard time discussing money because we shy away from it in polite company. You don't want to tell your best friend how much money you make, but you *have* to tell a client what to pay you if you want to keep working and putting food on the table. I have a challenge for you: after you name your price, stay quiet and let your client lead the rest of the conversation. It might be a long and uncomfortable silence, but it's important that you don't cave without the client even requesting a discount.

There is one major reason not to lower your rates immediately: it devalues what you bring to the table. A client who thinks you charge $40 but finds you willing to do it for $25 might assume that you are hard up for work which could be caused by an inability to deliver on your promises. There is something to be said for charging fairly for your services. The clients who mind paying a fair market value for your services likely aren't the kind of clients you want on your docket. If they try to barter with you over service rates, it could be a major red flag that tells you to run far away from this deal before you get burned. Even if they want you to do a trial piece for them, they should be willing to pay something or to get a smaller scope of work for free. Don't second-guess yourself when it comes to your prices. Be confident and your client will follow suit.

Invite Them to Create a Contract

AFTER YOU SHARE YOUR rates and give them a moment to respond to your price requests, you will be faced with a crossroads. How do you get from here (a prospective deal) to there (a closed deal at your desired pay rate)? The good news is it might be easier than you think to move ahead with a new job, and it takes just a little bit of practice. After you give your rates and allow them to respond, you will have a moment where you can either move forward with the project or decide a client isn't the right fit for you, financially or otherwise. If they are amenable to your rates and don't throw up any red flags that make you question how lucrative this work will be, you can invite them to create a contract with you so that everything is put in writing.

Upwork handles these contracts for them. All they have to do is click a few buttons and set up a few milestones. The rest is a piece of cake for both of you. You accept the contract and get started on the work as soon as possible. Communication stays in the platform via messages, voice calls, or video chats; money is exchanged in the platform; and deadlines are modified in the platform. Nothing happens off Upwork, so you can rest assured every detail of your project is recorded here. If you are on a call with a client, inviting them to make a contract and send you an offer is the next logical step.

If you are taking work outside of Upwork or are cold calling your clients from small local businesses, you might have a conversation that sounds more like this:

Freelancer: For a custom website, I charge $40 per hour and estimate that a site like yours will take approximately thirty hours to complete.

Silence

Client: That sounds reasonable.

Freelancer: Great! I would love to invite you to collaborate on this project with me. Would you like me to draw up a contract for our work or do you have a standard contract you would like to use?

This puts the ball back in the client's court and doesn't require you to wait awkwardly for them to make a decision about who or how to hire you. Some may have never worked with a freelancer in their lives, and they may not know what the next steps are. By inviting them to work with you, you give them a low-pressure way to commit to you. You are asking them a question, and they have the right to either lean into your suggestion or to tell you they need to think it over.

If they are ready to move forward, make sure every deadline and deliverable you discussed makes it into the writing of the contract. A standard template found online should be fine, but make sure you include a section for deliverables and pay rates. This offers you some protection in the event they default on what you are owed. Even if they come up with the contract, ensure there are clear guidelines on when and how you will be paid, as well as how much. If you make it this far, you are ready to get started on your very first job. You know what to charge and how to ensure you get paid the right amount and don't get cheated in the end.

The downside is not every job is one you want to take or add to your portfolio. Interviews with some clients will throw up some serious red flags, and there is a time and place to say no to work – no matter how much it may pay. Some clients will pay more because they know they are difficult to work with, and you will have to determine how you want to handle a difficult relationship with a client (if you want to deal with it at all). For some ideas of when you might want to say no to a client proposal for a contract, be sure to keep reading.

Unfortunately, not every job that comes your way is going to be a good fit for your skills, talents, and even your schedule. Some clients will be pushy and demanding, making it difficult to imagine what it would be like to work with them. The question is: how do you decide which jobs are going to be the right fit for you and which ones you should let fall by the wayside with a professional response that politely declines the offer? Here are some of the most obvious red flags that you may want to keep in mind when applying for jobs, communicating with new clients, and getting paid on time.

Requests for Free Work

THE FIRST AND PERHAPS most obvious reason to turn down a job is that the client expects you to do a lot of heavy lifting for no money. We already covered when and how to manage requests for free work, so we won't rehash it here. The important thing to note about clients who ask for free work is that they are *not* interested in getting a sample of your work to see if you are a good fit. Chances are, they are asking multiple freelancers to do slightly different tasks so they can cobble these efforts together to create a finished product.

If they aren't okay with seeing a small sample of your work, the odds are they aren't going to be happy with a full essay or a polished brochure either. Not to mention, you will have turned in the exact item they needed at the end of your "trial" and will be no closer to having a steady paycheck. Since you agreed to do this work for free, there is no recourse for you to receive payment even if they were happy with what you produced. There usually is no contract in place for free work because no money is going to be changing hands. As a result, your rates have little to no protection – and you have no guarantee of ongoing work. When clients request you work for no money, this should always send up a red flag. You may decide to ignore it and move ahead with a small sample, but I would caution you against giving away the entirety of the project without some form of payment protection or contract in place.

Expecting Deadlines without Paying

THIS ITEM IS CLOSELY related to the last section, but it warrants a header of its very own. On Upwork, you have something known as payment protection, a benefit to freelancers everywhere. To keep things simple, I'll summarize how it works here: First, a client sets up a milestone for you to submit some portion of the project to assess your progress and work quality. That milestone will show up under the contract on the platform and will have a monetary value assigned to it. When the client sets up the milestone, they will be asked to fund it or to place the funds within the milestone. They will be held in escrow until you submit the work for approval, and the client cannot remove the funds without notifying both the freelancer and Upwork.

They have fourteen days to review what you submitted. If a client fails to respond to your request for payment, Upwork automatically releases the funds after the fourteen-day hold. This prevents clients from ghosting you after you deliver the work in an attempt to hold off on paying for what you delivered. If a client refuses to fund a milestone before you commence work, this is a major red flag. They have some protection when it comes to holding their money in escrow, namely that they can dispute the quality of the work and request revisions before approving funds to be released. Because they don't have to release it until the work is delivered, they can rest easy knowing that their money is protected.

When you encounter a client who does not believe in funding milestones, you may also find that they have unclear expectations for when and how final work should be delivered. They hesitate to put it in writing because they know it will force their hand when it comes to paying you for a job well done. Take all of this combined as a sign that this client is not the best fit for you or your services. Never work without real money on the table. Digital marketplaces make it easier than ever to find work that satisfies you, but you never know who you are working with on the other side of the screen. Sketchy payment practices can burn you, so always prioritize payments with your clients first and foremost.

Unreasonable Communication Expectations

CHANCES ARE THAT YOU decided to embrace a freelance lifestyle because you wanted the freedom and flexibility it promises. That means that you may not spend the entirety of your nine-to-five sitting in an office chair. If you do, it is likely that you will spend that time working on other projects with more regularity. In other words, you likely spend your time pursuing the things that matter to you instead of sitting around and checking your email with alarming regularity. This poses a problem for some demanding clients who forget they may not be the center of your professional world. When you encounter one of these demanding clients, it should be a red flag that work is not going to be easy or smooth with them.

Think about your initial encounters with them as you hammer out the details of a contract. A video chat or a phone call may be the fastest way to get to the bottom of what deliverables you need to create for them, but some clients prefer the slower medium of email or messages within a freelancing platform so all communication is in writing. The problem is they want you to be as available for them as possible when they send missive after missive. It takes a long time for them to reply to your messages since you are rarely both online at the same time. However, they expect – and sometimes even demand – that you need to respond to them within the half-hour. If this sounds like a client you are thinking about working with, think again. You have better things to do than to check your email nonstop.

In fact, checking your email nonstop leads to lesser quality in your work because your attention is always divided. Every time you interrupt your deep, focused work in order to respond to yet another email, it will take you several minutes to get back into a flow state. Oftentimes, this is the perfect amount of time for your client to write you back, at which point you will have to start the process all over again. At the end of the day, you will likely find you didn't get as much done as you would have hoped for and you still may be no closer to hammering out the details of a new contract with that needy client. Suggest a quicker medium so you can both get to the bottom of things quickly and feel free to turn down the job if they say no and continue to demand emails as the only form of communication with unreasonable turnaround time expectations.

Inconvenient Times

THE BENEFIT OF THE freelance economy is that you can now work with people all over the globe and never leave your office. Opportunities abound in a global marketplace, but this comes with a set of problems all its own: can you work with clients in a different time zone? This is something you should consider when you start applying for jobs and communicating with clients. If you find that they want you to be available during their "business hours" but that aligns with the middle of the night for you, then the working relationship may start to break down. If they want you to schedule phone calls with them but those calls have to take place in the early dawn hours or well past your bedtime, then it might be a sign this relationship isn't going to work out long-term. You need to be able to live your life with the flexibility inherent to your freelancing schedule. For example, I rarely work with people on the West Coast because they are three hours behind. Most of my work takes place in the morning hours between 7:00 and 12:00. This translates to 4:00 to 9:00 for west coasters on Pacific time, which is often unrealistic.

In some cases, clients in other time zones may not pose a problem. Maybe you love working in the early morning or very late at night. Finding clients who share your affinity for these time slots or who are solidly in the middle of their day when those times roll around might be easier than you think. Because Upwork and Fiverr among others are all global platforms, it shouldn't be hard to find a time zone that corresponds with your desired working hours. Note early in the talks about a new project what time zone your client is in and when they might attempt to schedule a call with you to discuss the details. If it is too early or too late for you, it might be a bad fit.

Of course, this isn't to say that you *always* have to decline a job that doesn't align with a desired work schedule. Even I have been known to take jobs that exist outside of my East Coast time zone if it happens to be a project that I'm particularly excited about. I may take the initial phone call at a convenient time for the client to discuss the details, but I will also let them know about the time difference. If we can work through most of the details in one call and communicate via email from here on out (with some leeway for communication response time in my time zone), then I may still take the client on. This is something you will have to feel out on each contract but should be taken into consideration when booking a job.

How to Say No Professionally

NOW YOU HAVE SOME RED flags that clue you into the fact that a client may not be the right fit. What do you do if you know that a client is a poor fit and you need to gracefully back out of a contract before it even starts? It is never easy to explain to a client that they have thrown up some red flags and you are wary of working with them on any one project. I would argue that you should never actually tell them that you are declining them due to their own behavior as many people resist hearing something negative about themselves. Instead, you may want to try a different tactic that remains professional and detached while expressing your sympathy for not being able to work with them on this upcoming project.

Often, my go-to excuse is that I have booked up other work while we were going back and forth. This may even be true if a client has a hard time nailing down what they want to do with the project and sends me email after email or requires multiple phone calls to get to the bottom of their assignment. When I'm looking for new work, I often apply to five to ten jobs at a time and might start communications with three to four of those clients. By the time a client finally drills down into what they want or how they can communicate with me, I may have already booked another project.

My docket is on a first-come, first-served basis with an exception for recurring clients whom I am happy to take on at any point or refer to another freelancer if I have no time. This is often the easiest way to let a client down. I might say something like: "Unfortunately, my schedule is now full and I won't have the time to dedicate to your project as I had initially hoped. I wish you the best of luck in finding another writer who meets your needs!" Most people will not write back after this type of letter, but a few will. Some will be angry you have wasted their time without acknowledging the role they played by dragging their feet on issuing you an assignment to actually get started on. If you have been communicating with them too much to use this as an excuse at this juncture, being too busy to take on more client work isn't the only way to say no to a client.

In some cases, you might find that your skills simply aren't a good fit for the work assigned to you. When a situation like this comes to light, you need to be transparent with a potential client about your concerns regarding the job. For example, you may find that the style requested isn't a match for your personal writing or drawing style. Maybe they need a service that encompasses the skill set you have, but they also need an expansion on that service. To give you an example, this might look like a client who needs an e-book written and formatted. You may know how to write a great book but formatting isn't in your wheelhouse. You can be upfront about this mismatch of skills with your client and present them with two options: hire someone else to complete the entire project as described or split the work up between two (or more) freelancers. This can be as simple as saying: "I'm so excited about the opportunity to work with you on this project, but some of the services you need are outside my area of expertise. Would you be open to assigning some parts of this work to another freelancer who can better guide you through the process?"

Keep in mind that you never want to burn a bridge with someone who may turn out to be an excellent client for you in the future should their needs or communication style change. Even if you really do become too busy to work with them, the stars could align in the future for another project if you decline the current job with grace. Even though a potential client can't leave you a review on a freelancing platform without having assigned a contract to you, you should still make every effort to be kind and professional. Consider this practice at refining your negotiating chops as you branch out into more and more freelance work. Treating a prospective client with dignity now can reap its own reward well into the future. Even if they never use you for their own projects, they might know others they can refer to you for projects within your zone of genius, on a timeline that works for you, and with a communication style that doesn't bog you down.

With that business taken care of, it might be time to move on to the most important component of launching your freelance career: getting paid. As we covered here, there are some fail safes in place for getting paid on freelancing platforms like Upwork, but staying on top of things can help you get where you need to go. In the next chapter, we will dive into invoicing and getting paid on time so you always know you have money in the bank to pay your bills.

Invoicing and Getting Paid on Time

Is there anything worse than spending countless hours on a project and then finding your client drags their feet on issuing payment? Depending on how long it takes, you may begin to wonder if they intend to pay you at all. A lack of payment doesn't bode well for your bills, so you need to be sure you have enough runway to cover you in the event a client withholds payment for one reason or another. (Not sure what a runway is or how you can create one in your business? Be sure to see the second book in this series, *Finances for Freelancers*.) The good news is there is a lot you can do to reinforce good financial habits within your freelancing business and it all starts with the proper invoicing.

Invoice Promptly

AS SOON AS YOU SUBMIT the finished project to your client, it is time for them to pay up for the work completed to date. Some freelancers choose to wait around until they get final approval, but I think this sets everyone up for a disappointing experience. Once your client has the final product in hand, they can go ahead and use it for whatever their end goal is. They may not be inclined to review it quickly or to ask for revisions as promptly as you would like. You could spend days waiting for them to review it when they have gone ahead and used it as-is. Some freelancers may even find they wait weeks for approval when the client knows they were happy within the first 24 hours. This is an unsustainable model for your business.

Instead, you should prioritize sending out invoices to every client who receives a final copy of the project. When you send over the final document, whatever it may be, you should also attach a copy of the corresponding invoice. There are two real options for how to word your invoice: you could demand payment immediately upon receipt or you could give your client a certain amount of time to look over the work before issuing payment. Payment upon receipt is the most convenient way to manage your money as a freelancer because it ensures that you have stacks of cash in the bank and no outstanding invoices hanging out in limbo. However, you may choose to be a little more generous with your clients and offer payment terms like net 30 that give them a full month to review your work and then issue the payment. Of course, you can also set these payment terms to encompass whatever works best for you.

I would recommend sending your client something more official than simply a handwritten sheet of paper with your rate at the bottom. Invest some time in designing a template for invoices you can use from here on out. It should include your name, your logo if you have one, your preferred payment method and terms, and a line item for everything you are charging them for. Ideally, you would be able to save this as a PDF for them to access without giving them any ability to make changes to the file itself. Creating a template for your invoice should not take more than an hour, and it is something you can use again and again with minor modifications to the client's name section, the line items you are charging for, and even any differences in payment terms you have for specific clients. It might be a good idea to ask for a signature on the invoice for your file to prove the client received it.

If you are working on a freelance platform like Upwork, you can bypass this step of sending an invoice. Each project milestone you complete includes all of your payment protection. Instead of sending the draft or finished project to your client in a message, submit it through the milestone. This activates the escrowed funds in the milestone and starts the timer on the fourteen days your client has to review work and issue the payment. While it would be nice to be paid promptly, a two-week wait time may not be the end of the world. Make sure you have enough money in your account to cover your expenses if it will take you the full two weeks to receive payment. For those who don't know whether they have enough money to pay their bills or need help growing their savings account, you might want to see *Finances for Freelancers*.

Some jobs are not going to be billed on a per-project basis but rather on an hourly rate. If this describes your job, I recommend you don't wait until the end of the project to submit your hours unless the end of your project hits the two- to three-week mark for the final deliverable. This is often enough time for you to float your business financially until you can submit for your hours. Projects that extend past the two-week mark may require you to submit hours on a short-term basis. Usually, I submit my hours at the end of each week on the few contracts I have that work hourly. In some cases, I treat it the same as I did my nine-to-five job and submit my hours every two weeks if I know the client will pay promptly. This ensures I have a steady influx of money coming in on a predictable basis, just like the paycheck I used to collect from my office job.

Again, you can submit your hours as part of a general invoice typed up in Microsoft Word or Google Docs. Working on a freelance platform is a little different because you have two options for how hours are calculated: time-tracked hours or manual hours. Upwork allows clients to make sure you are actually working on their project during the hours you have allotted for it. They can see screenshots of your work, taken at random throughout the hours you are clocked in. This is not my preferred way to be paid because

I don't like to feel like someone is looking over my shoulder. I think the quality of my work speaks for itself and proves that I spent an adequate amount of time polishing it to perfection. This is why I vastly prefer being paid by the project so that I can take breaks without worrying about clocking in and out on an hourly basis.

The alternative is to submit manual hours where you tell the client when you worked and request payment. The downside to this method is that there is no payment protection for workers who choose to manually document their hours. It is easy for you to track your time on Upwork, but a client can't prove you actually worked the number of hours you claim. As a result, you might end up in a bitter dispute if they think you spent too much time for too few results. To combat this dispute which can ruin your chances of both getting paid and getting a positive review, I would recommend pricing your services in a package that gives your client access to a certain number of your hours for a flat rate. Make it a small package so they can evaluate your work at the outset and ensure everything is on track for the completion of their project, as they think it should go. A great starting point would be to package five to ten hours before an assessment of progress.

Follow Up

FREELANCERS OFTEN SHY away from the business side of their work, preferring the creativity of their chosen work. While working hard is certainly admirable, there comes a point where you need to be an entrepreneur first and foremost. (If you aren't sure that you can embrace being a business owner just yet, read the first book in this series *Freelance Freedom* to conquer the mindset shifts you need to succeed here.) That means you need to collect on the money you are owed and being shy about it isn't going to get you anywhere. Most of us have internalized the message that we do not want to talk about money in polite company. Unfortunately, this spells disaster for a business owner who needs money to keep the wheels on their company – even if it's just a company of one. Get ready to get uncomfortable if talking about money makes you feel sort of sick to your stomach. There is no easy way around asking for payment for your services.

Suppose that you sent your invoice to your client along with your finished work. If the work hasn't been officially finished yet, maybe you sent them a sample along with your biweekly hourly invoice that tallies up your hours toward a larger project. Either way, you submitted for payment and now your client has gone radio silent. Two approaches present themselves here: You can either forget about the invoice altogether or you can follow up.

New freelancers who give into imposter syndrome often take the first approach. They don't feel comfortable asking for money for a service they provide and feel their work isn't good enough to really get paid to do what they love. Instead of pinning the payment onto their client and making them responsible for the financial cost, they tend to put off talking about it, opting to keep their head down and keep working for no pay. I rarely say there is a *wrong* way to handle your business, but this is certainly one time where it is true. Clients who don't pay up should not get the priority treatment where you continue to work for them free of charge. There are times when a client who is typically punctual with payment may overlook your invoice or be out sick for a few days; these are the exceptions to the rule about letting invoices slide. Even if you do let them slide for a little while, you need to eventually bring them up with your clients in a follow-up.

When you are faced with a client who does not pay you promptly, you can keep working on the project – for a period of time. Depending on the scope of the project and exactly how much money they owe you, you may choose to work for a shorter or longer period. A client who does not even acknowledge you sent the request for payment might only warrant working for three or four more days before you reach out regarding your invoice. If they acknowledge they have received your invoice, it might be okay to wait a full week for them to review your progress and issue the payment. At the one-week mark, I would highly recommend following up with them about the invoice and halting the forward momentum of the project.

Why should you stop working when the one-week mark hits? First, you need to ensure your work is on the right track for what the client is looking to accomplish. You need their feedback before you spend another five, ten, or forty hours on their project only to be told it needs to go in a new and opposite direction. Second, you don't want to keep racking up hours if you aren't sure you are going to be paid for them at the end of the day. Nobody can work for free indefinitely and still keep their business running. Imagine what would happen if you had three, four, or more clients who refused to issue payments when invoices went out. Your rent can't be paid based on wishful thinking and sent invoices.

This is where the benefit of Upwork comes into the picture. If you choose to work for a fee on a project instead of hourly, you don't necessarily have to follow up with the client at all. Upwork automatically sends the payment through at the fourteen-day mark and you never have to send a single reminder that payment is due. Even if you work hourly, there is a little bit of protection built into the platform for you. After you log your hours, they get sent to the client for approval at the end of the week. This allows Upwork to take on the responsibility of following up on the hours you clocked and keeps you from having to send uncomfortable messages regarding payment. You may have to simply wait for the platform to work its magic when it comes to securing your pay.

How can you send a follow-up reminder for payment to your client without coming across as money-hungry? Certainly, there is a delicate balance here you need to consider carefully before you send a message. You don't want to sound as though you are only in this project for the paycheck, but you also need to convey that this is a bona fide business and you need to be paid for all services rendered. There are a couple of different ways you could phrase your request for the review of an invoice depending on the relationship you have with your client. I recommend doing all communication via email so you have a written account of your request for payment. Here are a couple of examples of ways you could phrase a request for payment:

I have really been enjoying working on your project these last few weeks and I'm proud of the progress we have made on it together. Last week, I sent over an invoice and an update on the status of the project, but I have not yet heard back from you. Can you confirm that you received that email and give me an update on how you think progress is going and when payment will be rendered? I look forward to hearing from you and finishing this project strong!

It has been a couple of weeks since I last heard from you, so I just wanted to reach out and touch base. We have an outstanding invoice for the last two weeks of hours, and I was hoping we could take care of this before I continue to move forward on the project. Please let me know a status update on payment as soon as possible so I can take care of my bookkeeping and clear out some of these pending invoices. Thanks for your time and attention to this matter!

Feel free to customize and tweak those responses until you land on something that feels right for you, your client, and your business. I always recommend leaving off on a positive note about how you are enjoying the work or how much you appreciate the business. It doesn't have to be anything effusive, but a little bit of a personal touch can go a long way with clients. You don't want it to read as if it were a form email you send out to all clients, so find unique ways to customize it for every project even if the same general message applies.

With all of this in mind, you are likely on your way to having a thriving freelancing business that makes enough money to cover your bills. Invoicing is an important component of making sure you get paid on time and can cover your costs. As you gain more experience, you should find that you are able to command a higher dollar amount for your services, no matter what area you focus your work on. Experience counts for a lot when it comes to setting your rates. Months and years after you first launch your business, you may want to consider raising your rates. To learn more about how to command more money commensurate with experience, the next chapter walks you through how to ask for what you deserve and navigate the waters of raising your rates with recurring clients.

When to Raise Your Rates

At the start of this book, we calculated how much you could reasonably charge for your services in line with market value and your overall level of experience. Now, we are coming to a close and it is time to address the elephant in the room: this initial rate you set for your work does *not* have to be the final price you land on months down the line. Pay should be commensurate with the level of experience a freelancer has under their belt. As you have started to tally up a list of clients who are satisfied with your work and are contributing to a robust portfolio of successful projects, you need to consider raising your rates.

There are two main benefits of raising your rates that can help you out financially. The first is obvious: the more money you make per hour or per project, the faster you can grow your savings accounts or investments. You might be able to offer yourself benefits through the business such as more sick days, vacation days, or even matching retirement savings funds out of company dollars. For those freelancers who are thinking about making a pivot, having a reliable source of income from one source gives you the flexibility to explore another avenue. The second is that you could stop working so many hours and achieve a greater work-life balance. At a higher rate, you can earn the same amount of money for fewer hours spent at your computer. Either way, there is abundant opportunity when it comes to earning more and furthering the lifestyle of your choice.

That being said, clients may not always be amenable to a rate hike that cuts into the bottom line of their own businesses. It might be the right move for your business, but it could cost you a client or two along the way. Here are a few guidelines to consider when it comes to raising your rates and how to communicate that to clients.

When to Raise Your Rates

IF YOU HAVE BEEN FOLLOWING along in this book up until now, you likely have already done the heavy lifting of figuring out how many hours it takes you to complete your bread-and-butter work. I will give you an example from my own freelancing experience: I know that it used to take me one hour to write a 500-word blog post for my very first client. Over the next six months of freelancing, I found that I could actually write 1,000 words per hour which effectively doubled the amount of work I could produce. If my client had been paying me hourly (which she did not), she would have gotten a fantastic deal: twice as much work for the same pay. Instead of getting one article every hour, she could now reliably double her output if she desired to do so but I would have been making *less* money because it was taking me *less* time. This is when a per-project fee comes into play.

Some freelancers start their careers off at an hourly rate because they need to probe a little deeper into how long it takes them to complete a project. Once you start to realize that your speed is increasing, it is time to switch to a project-based payment system that allows you to earn more for the same amount of work. This is easy enough to pitch to clients who are on an hourly model right now: simply tell them that you are changing your fee structure and will now be offering your services for a fixed fee. Take what you used to make and translate it into a per-project fee that makes sense for the work you provide. If you used to make $50 per hour and it took you two hours, then your project fee should be a minimum of $100 even if it only takes you one hour to complete it now. Do you see how this payment structure can really add up if you multiply it by ten, fifteen, or even twenty clients?

While your speed dictates one reason to consider changing your rates and fee structure, you may also choose to raise it based on your experience and the quality of the work you put out. At a certain point, you won't really be able to get any faster at your craft. After all, writers can only type so fast, translators can only read so quickly, and artists can only draw so many ideas per hour. This might sound like it sets you up for a price plateau, but you need to be mindful of how you can increase your payment moving forward in your freelancing career. Think of it this way: your day job gives you a raise during your annual review if you grow in experience, take on more challenging projects, and work as a great contributing member to the team as a whole. Why not put some of those same principles into practice and give yourself a raise at regular intervals if you have been learning and growing at your craft?

I would recommend setting annual dates with yourself where you can evaluate your rates and your skill level. If you spent this year leveling up in one area of your freelancing business, it might be time to start charging more for that particular skill. Maybe you have really grown as an artist or a writer. When your skill exceeds what you put out for your first few freelance projects, it might be time to consider giving yourself a raise. Expert freelancers who have highly specialized skills can command top dollar in the marketplace. There are always clients who want the best of the best to collaborate on their projects – and your rate is often an indicator of the quality of the work you put out. You may be the best person for the job, but if you charge the lowest rates, clients might be inclined to think you deliver subpar work. Consider what your rate says to the world at large and modify it if you find you only attract low-quality clients.

During your annual review, I want you to take an actual sample of your work from the very beginning of the year and compare it to your most recent sample. Is there a noticeable improvement in your skills? If there is, then it might be time to give yourself a raise. You can decide how much is reasonable based on your current rates. It might not be feasible to double your rates this year or even to give yourself a 50 percent raise. However, I do think you should raise your rates by more than a few cents an hour. A raise really only makes a difference when you have a dollar or two per hour more than you had before.

Depending on how much you were charging in the year up to this point, you might be able to give yourself even more than that. Do another market analysis and see what others are charging for services that are in line with what you offer and the quality that you provide. Make sure you are charging in line with the average and not lowballing yourself in an attempt to be covered up in work you don't really want or need. For freelancers who have been strategically underpricing their services in an attempt to underbid the competition and secure work, it is time to aim your sights a bit higher than this. Start charging fair market value for your services and clients will take notice of your business.

How to Tell Clients

THE BAD NEWS IS YOUR clients aren't going to want to hear you are raising your rates when they have come to rely on getting your services for rock-bottom prices. There is an easy way to weed out clients who aren't willing to increase your pay, but it might be uncomfortable for you at this juncture. To begin, I want to say that you need to honor the contracts you already have in place for the clients you booked. If you agreed to do a website redesign for $100, you can't raise your rates mid-project even if your annual review comes up in the midst or even at the start of the project. Honoring your word makes you a great business person and people will come to appreciate this about you. The simplest way to raise your rates is to just change them when a project ends. If the work isn't going to be recurring, you don't want to renew your contract, or you don't want to have an uncomfortable conversation about money, you can simply end the contract and bid at your new higher rate on subsequent jobs.

However, you will need to consider what needs to happen after this specific project ends before a new one begins if it is with a recurring client. A good way to handle this is to wait until the current project is almost finished and you know future work is on the table. You might give them a few weeks of advance notice to say that while you enjoy working with them, you will be changing your rates moving forward on the next project to whatever amount you have set in mind. While you would love to continue working with them, you understand if this is out of their budget and they need to find another freelancer who can deliver high-quality services at the same price point. Many clients would rather keep a known and more expensive freelancer on their team instead of braving the waters of unvetted freelancers who may not be able to deliver on their promises. An example of what you might say could look like this:

I've really enjoyed the work we have done on your project so far, which is why I wanted to write you as soon as possible. I will be raising my rates when our current project reaches its completion (or on whatever date, if the project is recurring) to $50 per project. I *understand that this might put my services outside of your price range, but I hope we can continue to work together well into the future. I look forward to finishing this project and to working with you further on upcoming projects!*

The key here is to be as direct as you possibly can and make no apologies for your rate increase. Like all workers, you are entitled to fair compensation for your work even as a freelancer. The companies and individuals who hire you are getting a great deal by not having to bring on a part-time or full-time employee which can be risky for their business and its bottom line. There is a difference between being sympathetic to their situation of losing out on a great deal and being apologetic for asking for the pay you deserve. I encourage you to try to strike a balance between these two opposing forces and always leave off on a hopeful and optimistic note about the work you will continue to do together in the future.

The only time you can come back to your client for more money on a project that is ongoing and has no clear end point is if there is a scope of work change. For example, your client might start out by asking you to write one article a week with two rounds of edits. Let's say that they no longer want two rounds of edits and have increased that number to four. This is known as scope creep and they should be charged accordingly for the extra services you are providing. If you feel that you have delivered on your end of the deal, then it makes sense to remind them of what your initial agreement was and give them a price if they want to continue with the new scope of work. On the other hand, you may absorb the cost if you feel it was your fault that the work wasn't as good as it could have been or if you misunderstood the directions. This is a delicate balance, but you will have to be honest with yourself and your client about where things went awry when it comes to insidious scope creep situations.

Final Thoughts

Pricing your services so that you can earn a profit is more art than science. It requires a detailed look at your personal finances as well as what you need to charge in order to cover your overhead costs of doing business. Not to mention, you have bill collectors banging on your door demanding rent, utilities, car insurance, and all of the other incidentals that come with living life in society these days. Setting your rates is arguably the most important aspect of making money in your new freelancing endeavor, but that doesn't make it easy. You will have to calculate and recalibrate your rates at various points throughout your journey. For now, it is enough to know that your business is capable of thriving if you follow some of these guidelines to pricing your services competitively in the market.

Throughout this book, I have included scripts of how you can communicate with your client more effectively. While you can take these templates and use them as-is, I encourage you to start to customize them for your unique business. You know how excellent your work is, what you have already done with your clients, and where things are falling apart. Be as specific as you can in your communication, but we will dive more into these topics in book four of the series surrounding how to communicate with and land your very first clients. If you are looking for templates about how you can talk with your clients about hard subjects, this next book will be packed full of them. This is the hard work that comes after setting your rates: running your business and keeping the wheels on it when client work starts to pile up – and it will start to pile up if you follow along in this entire series that walks you from startup to your first client.

I hope that you found this guide useful for setting realistic rates for your business from the very start, even before you start putting job proposals out there. If you need more help with your finances before you move into setting your rates, I highly recommend checking back in book two of the series, *Finances for Freelancers: Structure Your Business & Manage Your Money* and its corresponding workbook. It serves as a companion to this volume and can be helpful in pinpointing how much you need to make to cover your expenses. When you feel ready to start applying for jobs and are confident in what you can command price-wise on the market, it's time to take a closer look at what comes next for your business. It's time to move from your spot as a would-be freelancer to a thriving entrepreneur who knows what they have to offer is valuable. Start earning four, five, or even six figures from your freelancing business today!